TOUCHPOINTS™
for Recovery

Books in the
TOUCHPOINTS™
Series

TouchPoints™
FOR RECOVERY

TYNDALE HOUSE PUBLISHERS, INC.
CAROL STREAM, ILLINOIS

Visit Tyndale online at www.tyndale.com.

TYNDALE, New Living Translation, NLT, the New Living Translation logo, and Tyndale's quill logo are registered trademarks of Tyndale House Publishers, Inc.

TouchPoints is a trademark of Tyndale House Publishers, Inc.

TouchPoints for Recovery

Copyright © 2009 by Ronald A. Beers. All rights reserved.

Designed by Jennifer Ghionzoli

General editor: Jason D. Beers
Contributing writers: Ronald A. Beers, Rebecca Beers, Brian R. Coffey, Jonathan Farrar, Jonathan Gray, Sean A. Harrison, Sandy Hull, Amy E. Mason, Rhonda K. O'Brien, Douglas J. Rumford, Linda Taylor.

Scripture quotations are taken from the *Holy Bible,* New Living Translation, copyright © 1996, 2004, 2007 by Tyndale House Foundation. Used by permission of Tyndale House Publishers, Inc., Carol Stream, Illinois 60188. All rights reserved.

ISBN 978-1-4143-2023-6

Printed in the United States of America

17   16   15   14
9   8   7   6   5

INTRODUCTION

This little book is designed to help point you in the right direction on your journey to recovery. Desire is the feeling that feeds an addiction. The desires to relieve a withdrawal symptom, to relieve depression, or to experience the pleasure that comes from the rush an addictive substance produces are all temptations that are hard to walk away from. Does this mean that desire is a feeling that one must forego in order to recover? The answer is no. In fact, desire is a feeling one *must have* in order to recover. The Bible tells us of the strong desire felt by Jesus' disciples for their Savior, who helped them see life in a new light. This feeling of desire is what helped change these men's lives into positive and joyous ones filled with meaning and purpose. Are the Bible's words about Jesus' longing and willingness to help someone change his or her life still relevant today? Countless people whose lives have completely turned around will say yes. The road to recovery is not easy, but those who have looked to Jesus for help would all agree that their "new" lives began when they decided, or decided once again, to follow him. Their lives of pain, sadness, hurt, and unsatisfied desire stopped, and their lives of joy, meaning, purpose, and fulfilled desires began.

TouchPoints for Recovery has dozens of topics organized into helpful sections that take you step-by-step through the recovery process. Under each topic, you will find one or more questions that a person in recovery might want to ask. Below each question are Bible verses that help answer that question, plus a helpful note written by someone who has gone through the recovery process. We have chosen to first answer every question with words from the Bible itself because we believe that the Bible is God's written Word to all people. It is written exactly the way God wanted it to be written, so what better place to start than God's own words about how to live for him?

While we could not cover all topics, questions, and Scriptures related to the recovery process, our prayer is that this little book will give you a good start and that, along with this book, you will continue to deliberately search the Bible, seek wisdom from those who know how to help you, and find others who can teach you about the strength and determination we all need to follow God daily. Then you will grow closer to God and discover how his way of living is the path to real joy and satisfaction. Whether you read through this book page by page or whether you use it as a reference guide for topics of particular interest to you, may you find answers in God's Word as he longs to be your daily guide.

The editors

PSALM 40:2 | *[The Lord] lifted me out of the pit of despair, out of the mud and the mire. He set my feet on solid ground and steadied me as I walked along.*

EZEKIEL 36:26 | *[The sovereign Lord said,] "I will give you a new heart, and I will put a new spirit in you. I will take out your stony, stubborn heart and give you a tender, responsive heart."*

PHILIPPIANS 2:13 | *God is working in you, giving you the desire and the power to do what pleases him.*

COLOSSIANS 1:22 | *[God] has reconciled you to himself through the death of Christ. . . . As a result, he has brought you into his own presence, and you are holy and blameless as you stand before him without a single fault.*

2 TIMOTHY 3:16 | *All Scripture is inspired by God and is useful to teach us what is true and to make us realize what is wrong in our lives. It corrects us when we are wrong and teaches us to do what is right.*

CONTENTS

Part One

What We May Need to Recover From

ABUSE

How do I heal the wounds of abuse?

PROVERBS 24:29 | *Don't say, "Now I can pay them back for what they've done to me! I'll get even with them!"*

LAMENTATIONS 3:59 | *You have seen the wrong they have done to me, LORD. Be my judge, and prove me right.*

ROMANS 12:19 | *Never take revenge. Leave that to the righteous anger of God. For the Scriptures say, "I will take revenge; I will pay them back," says the LORD.*

EPHESIANS 4:31 | *Get rid of all bitterness, rage, anger, harsh words.*

If you have been a victim of abuse, you know that the hurt is real and that there are scars, both physical and emotional. When justice doesn't happen as it should, when life doesn't seem fair, that's when bitterness can consume you. But bitterness and the desire for revenge poison your own soul. It's essential to recognize and deal with the bitterness before it overwhelms you; otherwise, you might not be able to find healing and recover. You can be sure that God will bring justice. Leave that to him so you can focus on healing.

MATTHEW 5:43-44 | *[Jesus said,] "You have heard the law that says, 'Love your neighbor' and hate your enemy. But I say, love your enemies! Pray for those who persecute you!"*

MATTHEW 6:14-15 | *If you forgive those who sin against you, your heavenly Father will forgive you. But if you refuse to forgive others, your Father will not forgive your sins.*

LUKE 23:34 | *Jesus said, "Father, forgive them, for they don't know what they are doing."*

This may be the hardest act of the Christian life: forgiving those who have wronged you terribly without any expectation that they will change. Forgiveness is the only way to purge your soul of the toxins of bitterness and a vengeful spirit. When you forgive others, your heart is changed so you can move on. When you forgive, you are *not* saying that the hurt isn't real or that the event didn't matter or that you will put yourself in a position where you might be harmed again. Forgiving the abuser simply means that you refuse to let the abuser have any more control in your life. The person who hurt you doesn't even need to be told—the act of forgiveness occurs between you and God. Leave your hurt with God and allow his power to heal you from the inside so that you can recover.

PHILIPPIANS 4:8 | *Fix your thoughts on what is true, and honorable, and right, and pure, and lovely, and admirable. Think about things that are excellent and worthy of praise.*

As you fill your mind with good and pleasant thoughts of what your future can hold, you have less room and less time to dwell on the past. Focusing on the future will speed up your recovery time.

ADDICTION

How did I become addicted?

ROMANS 7:5 | *When we were controlled by our old nature, sinful desires were at work within us, and the law aroused these evil desires that produced a harvest of sinful deeds, resulting in death.*

2 PETER 2:19 | *You are a slave to whatever controls you.*

You became addicted when something started to control you. You probably didn't even realize it at the time. Do you remember when you started to skip important events or daily tasks in order to satisfy your urge "just this once" or "just one more time"? Addiction was developing at that point. Those who stop before they become addicted are the ones who recognize that if they don't control their urges, their lives are soon going to be controlled by something negative. Those who become addicted are the ones who *don't* recognize this.

Can addiction include more than substance abuse?

GENESIS 4:7 | *Watch out! Sin is crouching at the door, eager to control you. But you must subdue it and be its master.*

ROMANS 6:12, 14 | *Do not let sin control the way you live; do not give in to sinful desires. . . . Sin is no longer your master.*

ROMANS 8:6 | *Letting your sinful nature control your mind leads to death. But letting the Spirit control your mind leads to life and peace.*

1 CORINTHIANS 3:2-3 | *You still aren't ready, for you are still controlled by your sinful nature.*

The key to addiction is control—what controls you. You become a slave to something when it controls you. Anything can be controlling; thus addiction can be to anything. A few examples follow.

MATTHEW 19:21-22 | *Jesus [said], "If you want to be perfect, go and sell all your possessions and give the money to the poor, and you will have treasure in heaven. Then come, follow me." But when the young man heard this, he went away sad, for he had many possessions.*

Possessions can be addictive.

ROMANS 1:26-27 | *God abandoned them to their shameful desires. Even the women turned against the natural way to have sex and instead indulged in sex with each other. And the men, instead of having normal sexual relations with women, burned with lust for each other. Men did shameful things with other men, and as a result of this sin, they suffered within themselves the penalty they deserved.*

1 CORINTHIANS 6:18 | *Run from sexual sin! No other sin so clearly affects the body as this one does. For sexual immorality is a sin against your own body.*

GALATIANS 5:19 | *When you follow the desires of your sinful nature, the results are very clear: sexual immorality, impurity, lustful pleasures.*

Sexual immorality of all kinds can be addictive.

PROVERBS 20:1 | *Wine produces mockers; alcohol leads to brawls. Those led astray by drink cannot be wise.*

ISAIAH 5:11 | *What sorrow for those who get up early in the morning looking for a drink of alcohol and spend long evenings drinking wine to make themselves flaming drunk.*

Alcohol can be addictive.

JOB 22:24-25 | *If you give up your lust for money and throw your precious gold into the river, the Almighty himself will be your treasure.*

PROVERBS 11:28 | *Trust in your money and down you go!*

PROVERBS 21:17 | *Those who love pleasure become poor; those who love wine and luxury will never be rich.*

ECCLESIASTES 5:10 | *Those who love money will never have enough. How meaningless to think that wealth brings true happiness!*

Pleasure and wealth can be addictive.

JUDGES 14:12-13, 18-19 | *Samson said to them, "Let me tell you a riddle. If you solve my riddle during these seven days of the celebration, I will give you thirty fine linen robes and thirty sets of festive clothing. But if you can't solve it, then you must give me thirty fine linen robes and thirty sets of festive clothing." "All right," they agreed, "let's hear your riddle.". . . Before sunset of the seventh day, the men of the town came to Samson with their answer. . . . Samson . . . killed thirty men, took their belongings, and gave their clothing to the men who had solved his riddle. But Samson was furious about what had happened.*

PROVERBS 28:22 | *Greedy people try to get rich quick but don't realize they're headed for poverty.*

MATTHEW 27:35 | *After they had nailed [Jesus] to the cross, the soldiers gambled for his clothes by throwing dice.*

Gambling can be addictive.

1 CORINTHIANS 6:19-20 | *Don't you realize that your body is the temple of the Holy Spirit, who lives in you and was given to you by God? You do not belong to yourself, for God bought you with a high price. So you must honor God with your body.*

1 CORINTHIANS 10:31 | *Whether you eat or drink, or whatever you do, do it all for the glory of God.*

Drugs can be addictive. The Bible doesn't specifically mention the kind of drug addiction common today, but it does address the ever-present problem of putting things into your body that are harmful for it and that impair your ability to function.

PSALM 39:6 | *All our busy rushing ends in nothing.*

ECCLESIASTES 2:11 | *As I looked at everything I had worked so hard to accomplish, it was all so meaningless—like chasing the wind.*

ECCLESIASTES 5:3 | *Too much activity gives you restless dreams.*

Even work and busyness can be addictive.

What is the strongest addiction?

ISAIAH 59:1-2 | *Listen! The LORD's arm is not too weak to save you, nor is his ear too deaf to hear you call. It's your sins that have cut you off from God. Because of your sins, he has turned away and will not listen anymore.*

ROMANS 3:23 | *Everyone has sinned; we all fall short of God's glorious standard.*

ROMANS 6:16 | *Don't you realize that you become the slave of whatever you choose to obey? You can be a slave to sin, which leads to death, or you can choose to obey God, which leads to righteous living.*

GALATIANS 5:19-21 | *When you follow the desires of your sinful nature, the results are very clear: sexual immorality, impurity, lustful pleasures, idolatry, sorcery, hostility, quarreling, jealousy, outbursts of anger, selfish ambition, dissension, division, envy, drunkenness, wild parties, and other sins like these. Let me tell you again, as I have before, that anyone living that sort of life will not inherit the Kingdom of God.*

Sin is the most deeply ingrained addiction of every human being. In fact, it is the one addiction that every person who was ever born has struggled with, other than Jesus himself. Even though seeking help from a professional counselor is a good idea if you can't overcome an addiction on your own, no amount of help from spiritual or psychological counselors will cause you to stop sinning once and for all.

ISAIAH 1:18 | *"Come now, let's settle this," says the LORD. "Though your sins are like scarlet, I will make them as white as snow. Though they are red like crimson, I will make them as white as wool."*

ROMANS 6:6 | *We know that our old sinful selves were crucified with Christ so that sin might lose its power in our lives. We are no longer slaves to sin.*

ROMANS 6:18 | *You are free from your slavery to sin, and you have become slaves to righteous living.*

ROMANS 6:23 | *The wages of sin is death, but the free gift of God is eternal life through Christ Jesus our Lord.*

COLOSSIANS 1:22 | *[God] has reconciled you to himself through the death of Christ in his physical body. As a result, he has brought you into his own presence, and you are holy and blameless as you stand before him without a single fault.*

1 JOHN 1:9 | *If we confess our sins to him, he is faithful and just to forgive us our sins and to cleanse us from all wickedness.*

Ultimately, the only way to deal with your addiction to sin is to go to the One who has complete power over sin—Jesus Christ. When you asked Jesus to become your Savior, he literally gave you a new nature by sending his Holy Spirit to live in you. And when you ask him to take charge of your life and clean out the sin in you, he does several things: (1) he helps you want to stop sinning; (2) he gives you the strength to slow down the frequency of sin so that it doesn't control you; (3) he doesn't look at you as a sin addict anymore but instead sees you as holy; and (4) he promises that one day, when your body dies and you are brought to life with a new body in heaven, you will never have to deal with sin again.

Why is addiction so dangerous?

PROVERBS 5:22-23 | *An evil man is held captive by his own sins; they are ropes that catch and hold him. He will die for lack of self-control; he will be lost because of his great foolishness.*

ROMANS 1:28-29, 32 | *Since they thought it foolish to acknowledge God, he abandoned them to their foolish thinking and let them do things that should never be done. Their lives became full of every kind of wickedness, sin, greed, hate, envy, murder, quarreling, deception, malicious behavior, and gossip. . . .They know God's justice requires that those who do these things deserve to die, yet they do them anyway. Worse yet, they encourage others to do them, too.*

ROMANS 8:8 | *Those who are still under the control of their sinful nature can never please God.*

COLOSSIANS 1:20-21 | *Through [Christ] God reconciled everything to himself. . . . This includes you who were once far away from God. You were his enemies, separated from him by your evil thoughts and actions.*

Addictions are deceiving, destructive, and enslaving. They draw you away from God. This becomes dangerous because the further away from God you are, the harder it is for you to get back to him to receive his help. Don't separate yourself from the only One who can help you with your sin addiction.

Why can't I fight addictions by myself?

ROMANS 7:24-25 | *Oh, what a miserable person I am! Who will free me from this life that is dominated by sin and death? Thank God! The answer is in Jesus Christ our Lord. So you see how it is: In my mind I really want to obey God's law, but because of my sinful nature I am a slave to sin.*

PHILIPPIANS 2:13 | *God is working in you, giving you the desire and the power to do what pleases him.*

JAMES 1:14 | *Temptation comes from our own desires, which entice us and drag us away.*

You can't fight addictions by yourself because all you have to draw on is your sinful nature. Learning to trust God to help you overcome addiction is hard, but it is worth the effort. Start by telling God that you cannot do this on your own and that you need help. Ask him to teach you to trust him, and he will.

ECCLESIASTES 4:9-10, 12 | *Two people are better off than one, for they can help each other succeed. If one person falls, the other can reach out and help. But someone who falls alone is in real trouble. . . . A person standing alone can be attacked and defeated, but two can stand back-to-back and conquer. Three are even better, for a triple-braided cord is not easily broken.*

MARK 6:7 | *[Jesus] called his twelve disciples together and began sending them out two by two.*

Jesus created accountability by sending his disciples out in pairs. This is a wise practice to imitate because a person standing alone against the world is vulnerable. People need mutual support, companionship, and encouragement. You can get these things from relationships with others who will challenge you to stay on the right path.

If I shouldn't let anything control me, why then should I submit to God?

ROMANS 6:14, 18 | *Sin is no longer your master, for you no longer live under the requirements of the law. Instead, you live under the freedom of God's grace. . . . Now you are free from your slavery to sin, and you have become slaves to righteous living.*

2 CORINTHIANS 3:17 | *The Lord is the Spirit, and wherever the Spirit of the Lord is, there is freedom.*

GALATIANS 5:22-23 | *The Holy Spirit produces this kind of fruit in our lives: love, joy, peace, patience, kindness, goodness, faithfulness, gentleness, and self-control.*

It might seem like a bad idea to let God take over your life if you have been controlled by something else for a while. After all, doesn't it seem right to be free from things that are controlling? But God's control is the only kind of control that produces completely positive results. When you learn to trust God and ask him to help you live your life, he will help you become free of the things that make you unhappy and the addictions that keep you chained to bad habits. This is because God knows what will make your life satisfying. He really does. It is only through trust in his guidance that you will become truly free to experience all God meant for you to enjoy.

How do I ask God to help me be free from an addiction?

PSALM 19:13 | *Keep your servant from deliberate sins! Don't let them control me. Then I will be free of guilt and innocent of great sin.*

EZEKIEL 36:26 | *[The sovereign Lord said,] "I will give you a new heart, and I will put a new spirit in you. I will take out your stony, stubborn heart and give you a tender, responsive heart."*

1 CORINTHIANS 10:13 | *The temptations in your life are no different from what others experience. And God is faithful. He will not allow the temptation to be more than you can stand. When you are tempted, he will show you a way out so that you can endure.*

JAMES 4:7, 10 | *Humble yourselves before God. Resist the devil, and he will flee from you. . . . Humble yourselves before the Lord, and he will lift you up in honor.*

It is understandable that you don't fully trust God yet. You wonder where he was when you were walking through your dark valley. It is hard to trust anyone after being addicted to something for some time. But if you sincerely ask God to teach you to trust him, he will grant your request. As soon as you realize that you can trust the Lord to guide you out of addiction, he will help you do this. He will give you the strength to resist temptation and the will to live free of it. This doesn't mean you won't need the help of a counselor as well (because God often works through others to help bring healing—doctors, counselors, nutritionists), but first you need God's healing power to help you want to change.

How can I forget about the feeling that my addiction gives me?

ROMANS 8:6 | *Letting your sinful nature control your mind leads to death. But letting the Spirit control your mind leads to life and peace.*

ROMANS 15:13 | *I pray that God, the source of hope, will fill you completely with joy and peace because you trust in him. Then you will overflow with confident hope through the power of the Holy Spirit.*

2 CORINTHIANS 5:17 | *Anyone who belongs to Christ has become a new person. The old life is gone; a new life has begun!*

To say that addictions don't feel good would be a lie. It can feel great to be "high" on something, which is why people become addicted. Drugs or alcohol can take you away to a place where you forget trouble and pain. However, there are limits with this kind of high: It is temporary, and it is artificial (not to mention dangerous). Chasing after the feeling that drugs or alcohol gives you gets tiring and boring because the high gets less exciting each time and you need more of your substance of choice to get high. This is very different from the natural, spiritual high that you can get from a relationship with God. When those who are trusting in God explain this high, addicts may feel these people are naive, but those who are trusting in God may feel addicts explaining *their* high are naive. Keep in mind that thousands every day turn away from their addiction and turn to God, and they explain their new feeling as something they wish they had discovered a long time ago. This new high that you can get from God is absolutely real because it is his Holy Spirit who literally becomes a part of you and reveals to you what real joy, real love, and real satisfaction are. You will find everything you've been searching for—and it will be lasting and genuine and completely safe.

BURNOUT

How do I prevent and recover from burnout?

1 KINGS 18:46 | *The LORD gave special strength to Elijah.*

1 CHRONICLES 16:11 | *Search for the LORD and for his strength; continually seek him.*

2 CHRONICLES 16:9 | *The eyes of the LORD search the whole earth in order to strengthen those whose hearts are fully committed to him.*

PSALM 22:15, 19 | *My strength has dried up like sunbaked clay. . . . O LORD, do not stay far away! You are my strength; come quickly to my aid!*

ZECHARIAH 4:6 | *It is not by force nor by strength, but by my Spirit, says the LORD of Heaven's Armies.*

Sometimes you can't stop working, even though you're exhausted and you long for time off to get your act together. When you need to finish a job but feel you don't have the strength to keep going, you are going to have to find strength from a higher power—God. So pray to him for enough strength to reach a stopping point or to last until the job is completed. There is a strength that only God can give, and you can receive it by asking. And many times you can prevent burnout by planning ahead so you don't take on more than is reasonable.

EXODUS 18:21-23 | *[Moses' father-in-law said to Moses,] "Select . . . some capable, honest men. . . . They will help you carry the load, making the task easier for you. If you follow this advice . . . then you will be able to endure the pressures."*

Try to find others who are willing to help you with your workload. This can ease the stress on you as you finish your task and then work on recovering.

EXODUS 23:12 | *You have six days each week for your ordinary work, but on the seventh day you must stop working.*

When you are tired, your productivity decreases dramatically. Rest refreshes and energizes you to be more productive. Regular, consistent, weekly rest is an important part of avoiding and recovering from burnout. Recognizing your limits is essential. Maybe you are trying to do too much and becoming discouraged when nothing seems to go right.

2 SAMUEL 17:28-29 | *They brought sleeping mats, cooking pots, serving bowls, wheat and barley, flour and roasted grain, beans, lentils, honey, butter, sheep, goats, and cheese for David and those who were with him. For they said, "You must all be very hungry and tired and thirsty after your long march through the wilderness."*

1 KINGS 19:5-8 | *As [Elijah] was sleeping, an angel touched him and told him, "Get up and eat!" . . . So he ate and drank and lay down again. Then the angel of the LORD came again and touched him and said, "Get up and eat some more, or the journey ahead will be too much for you." So he got up and ate and drank, and the food gave him enough strength to travel.*

Poor nutrition and poor health habits invite burnout. Take good care of your body by exercising, resting, and eating nutritious meals while you are working hard and during your period of recovery.

DAMAGED RELATIONSHIPS ——•●

What does the Bible say about reconciliation between people?

MATTHEW 5:23-24 | *If you are presenting a sacrifice at the altar in the Temple and you suddenly remember that someone has something against you, leave your sacrifice there at the altar. Go and be reconciled to that person. Then come and offer your sacrifice to God.*

It is important to be reconciled to others before you present yourself to God. He wants a clean heart and clean hands when you come to him to worship.

MATTHEW 5:25-26 | *When you are on the way to court with your adversary, settle your differences quickly. Otherwise, your accuser may hand you over to the judge, who will hand you over to an officer, and you will be thrown into prison. And if that happens, you surely won't be free again until you have paid the last penny.*

Working for reconciliation with others is important to your own welfare.

MATTHEW 18:15 | *If another believer sins against you, go privately and point out the offense. If the other person listens and confesses it, you have won that person back.*

God wants you to resolve your differences with others to retain friendships.

How can I mend a broken relationship with a friend?

EPHESIANS 4:32 | *Be kind to each other, tenderhearted, forgiving one another, just as God through Christ has forgiven you.*

COLOSSIANS 3:13 | *Make allowance for each other's faults, and forgive anyone who offends you. Remember, the Lord forgave you, so you must forgive others.*

Reconciliation requires someone to take a first step of kindness. It requires you to make the decision to forgive and show mercy.

1 SAMUEL 25:28 | *Please forgive me if I have offended you in any way.*

PROVERBS 18:19 | *An offended friend is harder to win back than a fortified city.*

LUKE 15:18 | *I will go home to my father and say, "Father, I have sinned against both heaven and you."*

2 CORINTHIANS 2:5-7 | *I am not overstating it when I say that the man who caused all the trouble hurt all of you more than he hurt me. Most of you opposed him, and that was punishment enough. Now, however, it is time to forgive and comfort him. Otherwise he may be overcome by discouragement.*

Forgiveness is both a decision and a process. Sometimes you must decide to forgive whether you feel like it or not. Although making amends for an offense is difficult, your relationships with others are worth your immediate and diligent efforts. Saying "I'm sorry" is very important. When you have hurt someone, apologize as quickly as possible and make any needed restitution.

Can I get past the bitterness I feel from divorce?

MARK 11:25 | *When you are praying, first forgive anyone you are holding a grudge against, so that your Father in heaven will forgive your sins, too.*

EPHESIANS 4:31-32 I *Get rid of all bitterness . . . forgiving one another, just as God through Christ has forgiven you.*

HEBREWS 12:15 I *Watch out that no poisonous root of bitterness grows up to trouble you, corrupting many.*

If you are a victim of divorce, you may have been hurt badly; you may have been treated unjustly; you may have been humiliated. But bitterness, allowed to fester and grow, will overshadow all you do. Only forgiveness can get rid of bitterness. Once bitterness is not an issue, you will be free to live as a happier person.

COLOSSIANS 1:8 I *[Paul said,] "[Epaphras] has told us about the love for others that the Holy Spirit has given you."*

1 THESSALONIANS 3:12 I *May the Lord make your love for one another and for all people grow and overflow, just as our love for you overflows.*

1 THESSALONIANS 4:9 I *We don't need to write to you about the importance of loving each other, for God himself has taught you to love one another.*

After trust is broken and divorce occurs, it may be hard to allow yourself to love again. But God is love. The more you appreciate and understand just how much he loves you, regardless of what you have done or what others have done to you, the more his love can overflow to others, and the easier it will be to move on.

Will God forgive my past sins—even sexual sin? Can he fully accept me?

ACTS 13:38-39 I *Through this man Jesus there is forgiveness for your sins. Everyone who believes in him is declared right with God.*

God will forgive any sin if there is sincere repentance, a desire to stop that sin and a desire for forgiveness.

ROMANS 1:24 | *God abandoned them to do whatever shameful things their hearts desired. As a result, they did vile and degrading things.*

God will not forgive sin when you persist in that sin and are not sorry about it. Engaging in persistent, willful sin shows that there is no repentance and that you care more about pleasing yourself than pleasing God. But honest confession of your sins results in full forgiveness and restored fellowship with God.

I am the victim of incest, and I feel so ashamed and so angry. How can I ever recover?

PSALM 12:5 | *The LORD replies, "I have seen violence done to the helpless, and I have heard the groans of the poor. Now I will rise up to rescue them, as they have longed for me to do."*

PSALM 22:24 | *[The Lord] has not ignored or belittled the suffering of the needy. He has not turned his back on them, but has listened to their cries for help.*

PSALM 34:18 | *The LORD is close to the brokenhearted; he rescues those whose spirits are crushed.*

PROVERBS 22:8 | *Those who plant injustice will harvest disaster, and their reign of terror will come to an end.*

HABAKKUK 1:2, 13 | *How long, O LORD, must I call for help? But you do not listen! "Violence is everywhere!" I cry, but you do not come to save. . . . But you are pure and cannot stand the sight of evil. Will you wink at their treachery? Should you be silent while the wicked swallow up people more righteous than they?*

Understandably, you may be feeling angry, betrayed, ashamed, hurt, vengeful, brokenhearted, desolate, and/or violated. And you may be angry at God for not stopping the abuse. For now, you won't know why God prevents some acts of violence and not others. But know that God detests all acts of violence and that he longs to bring you emotional and physical healing. If you run to him for help, you will find healing and recovery.

DEPRESSION/SADNESS

What can I do when I'm depressed? How can I recover?

PSALM 42:5-6 | *Why am I discouraged? Why is my heart so sad? I will put my hope in God! I will praise him again—my Savior and my God! Now I am deeply discouraged, but I will remember you.*

Depression can be a time for soul searching, for asking questions. It may come as a result of overwhelming circumstances or simply from concentrating on unpleasant ones. When you ask the questions the psalmist asked, then your focus changes to God, who can help you through any circumstance and who will stay with you until he finally rescues you from your last discouraging moment. Praise God for how he has rescued his people in the past, and trust that he will rescue you now and in the future. It is possible he may do this through a professional or medical counselor who is trained to help those who are suffering from sadness, grief, or clinical depression.

MATTHEW 26:39, 42, 44 | *[Jesus prayed,] "I want your will to be done, not mine." . . . Then Jesus . . . prayed, "My Father! If this cup cannot be taken away unless I drink it, your will be done." . . . [Then] he went to pray a third time, saying the same things again.*

ACTS 16:22-23, 25 | *A mob quickly formed against Paul and Silas, and the city officials ordered them stripped and beaten with wooden rods. They were severely beaten, and then they were thrown into prison. . . . Around midnight Paul and Silas were praying and singing hymns to God, and the other prisoners were listening.*

Be persistent in prayer. There are countless examples in the Bible as well as today of God lifting a burden from someone who kept trusting him through persistent prayer. As you meet with God in prayer and with an open Bible, you welcome him to do his work of comfort, transformation, and encouragement—often in ways you cannot explain. Never underestimate God's willingness to give peace, hope, and personal victory in your life.

PSALM 35:10 | *With every bone in my body I will praise him: "LORD, who can compare with you? Who else rescues the helpless?"*

PSALM 103:1-4 | *Let all that I am praise the LORD; with my whole heart, I will praise his holy name. Let all that I am praise the LORD; may I never forget the good things he does for me. He forgives all my sins. . . . He redeems me from death and crowns me with love and tender mercies.*

PSALM 145:3 | *Great is the LORD! He is most worthy of praise!*

Although it is hard to do when you feel depressed, praising the Lord lifts your mood almost immediately, even if just a little. You don't have to act extremely happy or dance in order to praise God. If you notice something awesome such as a beautiful sunset, or if you remember things he has given you in the past, give him a quick praise or thanks, and your mood will lift. Praise the Lord for his unfailing, unconditional love for you. Praise him for the gift of salvation and eternal life. Praise him for anything good you see around you. Praise him for his promise to help you through your depression. Your praises are deliberate acts of obedience that, while difficult sometimes, produce almost immediate results.

Can any good come out of my depression?

NEHEMIAH 8:10 | *Don't be dejected and sad, for the joy of the LORD is your strength!*

PSALM 126:5 | *Those who plant in tears will harvest with shouts of joy.*

2 CORINTHIANS 12:9 | *[The Lord] said, "My grace is all you need. My power works best in weakness." So now I am glad to boast about my weaknesses, so that the power of Christ can work through me.*

When you are weak and in need, you are more open to receive God's strength. When everything is going your way, it's easy to overlook God's hand in your life. As God works through your weakness, however, you learn to depend more on him and learn to recognize and be grateful for the good work that he can accomplish in you. Then, when you come out on the other side of your depression, you find yourself closer to God and stronger than ever.

Does feeling depressed mean something is wrong with my faith?

PSALM 35:9 | *I will be glad because [the Lord] rescues me.*

PSALM 40:2 | *He lifted me out of the pit of despair, out of the mud and the mire. He set my feet on solid ground and steadied me as I walked along.*

MATTHEW 14:30-31 | *When [Peter] saw the strong wind and the waves, he was terrified and began to sink. "Save me, Lord!" he shouted. Jesus immediately reached out and grabbed him. "You have so little faith," Jesus said. "Why did you doubt me?"*

God wants to begin the work of lifting you out of the pit of depression and fear, but you must let him. There is something wrong with your faith only if you convince yourself that God cannot or does not want to help you.

What does God say about suicide?

GENESIS 1:27 | *God created human beings in his own image. In the image of God he created them; male and female he created them.*

1 CORINTHIANS 6:20 | *God bought you with a high price. So you must honor God with your body.*

Life at times can be especially difficult. You may feel abandoned, you may have lost everything, or you may be burdened with a load of guilt. But even in times when death seems to be the only way out, it is important to remember that you have already been promised victory in your troubles through Jesus Christ. Although the Bible gives us reasons not to fear death, you should never try to end your own life. Ending life, the most precious gift from God, deeply offends him by destroying his very own creation. You need to seek peace with God; although the troubles may not end immediately, you will find the strength to live.

PSALM 139:13-16 | *You made all the delicate, inner parts of my body and knit me together in my mother's womb. Thank you for making me so wonderfully complex! Your workmanship is marvelous—how well I know it. You watched me as I was being formed in utter seclusion, as I was woven together in the dark of the womb. You saw me before I was born. Every day of my life was recorded in your book. Every moment was laid out before a single day had passed.*

JEREMIAH 1:4-5 | *The LORD gave me this message: "I knew you before I formed you in your mother's womb. Before you were born I set you apart and appointed you as my prophet to the nations."*

These words are not just nice poetry—they are inspired words that describe God's creation of each individual. Every person ever born was known by God before his or her birth. Human beings are God's workmanship, created by God for a purpose. Human lives are God's to create and God's to end. Suicide is making a decision to end a life, a decision that is God's alone.

How can I deal with thoughts I have about suicide?

MATTHEW 28:20 | *[Jesus said,] "Be sure of this: I am with you always, even to the end of the age."*

When death seems to be the only answer, it is important to remember that you are not alone on this earth. Even when it seems everyone else has abandoned you, God is by your side, ready to comfort and help you.

JEREMIAH 1:5 | *[The Lord said,] "I knew you before I formed you in your mother's womb. Before you were born I set you apart and appointed you as my prophet to the nations."*

JEREMIAH 29:11 | *"I know the plans I have for you," says the LORD. "They are plans for good and not for disaster, to give you a future and a hope."*

When you are tempted by thoughts of hopelessness, remember that God created you for a reason. He has planned a bright future and will help you get there, even though it may lead through some dark times.

DEUTERONOMY 4:29 | *You will search again for the LORD your God. And if you search for him with all your heart and soul, you will find him.*

If you look for God, you will find him. He loves you and has a purpose for you.

JOSHUA 1:9 | *Be strong and courageous! Do not be afraid or discouraged. For the LORD your God is with you wherever you go.*

Do you ever feel that life is a battle and that you are losing? Life can be very discouraging. When you are tired or when the obstacles seem too big, it is easy to lose hope. Remember that as a believer you have God's Spirit in you, and you can tap into God's almighty power. You don't have to win the battle on your own—God doesn't even want you to try. When you ask for his help in your struggles, God will fight for you.

DISCOURAGEMENT

How can I recover from discouragement?

1 KINGS 19:10 | *[Elijah said,] "I am the only one left, and now they are trying to kill me, too."*

PSALM 25:16-18 | *Turn to me and have mercy, for I am alone and in deep distress. My problems go from bad to worse. Oh, save me from them all! Feel my pain and see my trouble. Forgive all my sins.*

1 PETER 5:8-9 | *Watch out for your great enemy, the devil. He prowls around like a roaring lion, looking for someone to devour. Stand firm against him, and be strong in your faith. Remember that your Christian brothers and sisters all over the world are going through the same kind of suffering you are.*

When you are discouraged, you feel sorry for yourself. This feeling often becomes addicting because self-pity unexplainably feels good. However, don't let it get a hold on you, for it leads down a path to depression and destruction. Guard against thinking you are the only one who is going through troubles—it is encouraging to realize others are going through similar trials.

PSALM 55:22 | *Give your burdens to the LORD, and he will take care of you.*

PSALM 142:3 | *When I am overwhelmed, you alone know the way I should turn.*

MATTHEW 11:28 | *Jesus said, "Come to me, all of you who are weary and carry heavy burdens, and I will give you rest."*

Let God carry your burdens when they are too heavy. This doesn't mean he will take all your problems away or that he will solve your problems for you. That happens in heaven. But for now, God promises to give you wisdom, strength, comfort, and discernment to help you.

NEHEMIAH 4:10, 14 | *The people of Judah began to complain, "The workers are getting tired, and there is so much rubble to be moved. We will never be able to build the wall by our-selves." . . . As I looked over the situation, I called together the . . . people and said to them, "Don't be afraid of the enemy! Remember the Lord, who is great and glorious, and fight for your brothers, your sons, your daughters, your wives, and your homes!"*

ROMANS 12:6 | *God has given us different gifts for doing certain things well.*

1 CORINTHIANS 15:58 | *Be strong and immovable. Always work enthusiastically for the Lord, for you know that nothing you do for the Lord is ever useless.*

GALATIANS 6:9 | *Let's not get tired of doing what is good. At just the right time we will reap a harvest of blessing if we don't give up.*

When you are discouraged, try to remember the things you are passionate about. Why do you have these passions? You might not know at the time how you will use them, but God gave you gifts and interests for a reason. Knowing this—and knowing that the more involved you are with your passions, the more fulfilled you will be—will give you encouragement.

What can I do when my situation seems hopeless?

1 SAMUEL 1:10 | *Hannah was in deep anguish, crying bitterly as she prayed to the LORD.*

You can pray. In the midst of Hannah's hopelessness, she prayed to God, knowing that if any hope was to be found, it would be found in him.

ACTS 16:24-25 | *The jailer put them into the inner dungeon and clamped their feet in the stocks. Around midnight Paul and Silas were praying and singing hymns to God, and the other prisoners were listening.*

You can worship. Paul and Silas were on death row for preaching about Jesus, yet in this seemingly hopeless situation, they sang praises to God. Why? Because of their hope in Jesus' promise to always be with them (see Matthew 28:20).

PROVERBS 10:28 | *The hopes of the godly result in happiness, but the expectations of the wicked come to nothing.*

You can focus on eternity. No matter how hopeless things seem here on earth, in Jesus you have ultimate, eternal hope. Those who know him have been promised a joyful future in heaven for eternity. There is much more living to do beyond the grave.

How can I get past my insecurity and accept myself?

PSALM 8:4-5 | *What are mere mortals that you should think about them, human beings that you should care for them? Yet you made them only a little lower than God and crowned them with glory and honor.*

PSALM 139:17 | *How precious are your thoughts about me, O God. They cannot be numbered!*

MATTHEW 10:29-31 | *What is the price of two sparrows—one copper coin? But not a single sparrow can fall to the ground without your Father knowing it. And the very hairs on your head are all numbered. So don't be afraid; you are more valuable to God than a whole flock of sparrows.*

Remind yourself how valuable you are to God. He made you just as you are for a specific purpose.

PROVERBS 15:22 | *Plans go wrong for lack of advice; many advisers bring success.*

PROVERBS 19:20 | *Get all the advice and instruction you can, so you will be wise the rest of your life.*

PROVERBS 27:9 | *The heartfelt counsel of a friend is as sweet as perfume and incense.*

1 CORINTHIANS 12:8 | *To one person the Spirit gives the ability to give wise advice; to another the same Spirit gives a message of special knowledge.*

Get help from friends, your pastor, or a professional counselor if you can't seem to get on top of your insecurity. There is a certain healing that comes to you when you share your troubles with others.

GRIEF

How do I get over grief?

GENESIS 50:1 | *Joseph threw himself on his father and wept over him.*

2 SAMUEL 18:33 | *The king was overcome with emotion. He . . . burst into tears. And . . . he cried, "O my son Absalom! My son, my son Absalom!"*

ECCLESIASTES 3:1, 4 | *For everything there is a season, a time for every activity under heaven. . . . A time to cry and a time to laugh. A time to grieve and a time to dance.*

Recognize that grieving after a loss is necessary and important. You need to give yourself that freedom. Taking time to grieve is an important part of healing because it allows you to release the emotional pressure of your sorrow.

ISAIAH 43:2 | *When you go through deep waters, I will be with you. When you go through rivers of difficulty, you will not drown. When you walk through the fire of oppression, you will not be burned up; the flames will not consume you.*

LAMENTATIONS 3:20-22 | *I will never forget this awful time, as I grieve over my loss. Yet I still dare to hope when I remember this: The faithful love of the LORD never ends! His mercies never cease.*

1 PETER 1:7 | *When your faith remains strong through many trials, it will bring you much praise and glory and honor on the day when Jesus Christ is revealed to the whole world.*

When you are faced with great adversity or grief, you probably ask, "Where is God when I need him most?" The answer is always the same—he is right beside you. God is there with the power to help you cope. In this life, God doesn't promise to save you *from* trouble. In fact, the verse from Isaiah says "*when* you go through deep waters," assuming that adversity will come your way. It's the natural consequence of living in a broken world. God does not give you everything you want, because then you would follow him for the wrong reasons and your character would never grow. Instead, God promises to be with you *in* your troubles, to give you wisdom to cope, and to strengthen you as you learn to deal with and overcome adversity.

REVELATION 21:4 | *He will wipe every tear from their eyes, and there will be no more death or sorrow or crying or pain. All these things are gone forever.*

Many times, thinking about heaven will help you overcome grief. With the realization that there is no grief in heaven, you will gain hope that someday life will be much, much better.

MARK 14:34 | *[Jesus told his disciples,] "My soul is crushed with grief to the point of death. Stay here and keep watch with me."*

At times Jesus needed to be alone with his grief, and at times he sought others to share in his grief. He expressed his emotions honestly. Like Jesus, explain your feelings to others. Find someone you trust who will listen to what you have to say, and then share your feelings with him or her. You will be relieved and refreshed.

GUILT

How can I be free from guilt?

PSALM 19:12-13 | *Cleanse me from these hidden faults. Keep your servant from deliberate sins! Don't let them control me. Then I will be free of guilt.*

JEREMIAH 3:13 | *Only acknowledge your guilt. Admit that you rebelled against the LORD your God.*

ROMANS 3:23-24 | *Everyone has sinned; we all fall short of God's glorious standard. Yet God, with undeserved kindness, declares that we are righteous. He did this through Christ Jesus when he freed us from the penalty for our sins.*

Guilt comes from the act of doing something wrong. Since no one is perfect and you cannot avoid sinning altogether, you will always have guilt. That is, unless you confess your sins to God and to those whom you sinned against. This is the only way to free yourself from the burdens that guilt puts on you. Getting rid of guilt is one of the major steps in recovery because this gives you the freedom to move ahead with a fresh start.

How do I handle feelings of guilt that linger even after I have confessed my sin?

PSALM 51:7 | *Purify me from my sins, and I will be clean; wash me, and I will be whiter than snow.*

ACTS 13:39 | *Everyone who believes in [Jesus] is declared right with God.*

Guilt disappears when you are forgiven. Most of what you feel, if you have confessed your sins to God and others, is probably shame and regret over what you have done or the lingering consequences of your actions. Along with confessing your sins, you need to ask God to help you get rid of your shame and regret as well.

PAST

Can I live a healthy, godly life in spite of my past?

PSALM 143:5 | *I remember the days of old. I ponder all your great works and think about what you have done.*

ISAIAH 1:18 | *"Come now, let's settle this," says the LORD. "Though your sins are like scarlet, I will make them as white as snow. Though they are red like crimson, I will make them as white as wool."*

GALATIANS 1:13, 15 | *[Paul said,] "You know what I was like when I followed the Jewish religion—how I violently persecuted God's church. I did my best to destroy it. . . . But even before I was born, God chose me and called me by his marvelous grace."*

PHILIPPIANS 3:13 | *I focus on this one thing: Forgetting the past and looking forward to what lies ahead.*

Your memories of the past are like a photo album containing snapshots of your life. These snapshots are not just of happy moments and celebrations; they also record failures, tragedies, and acts of deepest shame. You, like most people, would like to lock some of your past away or tear out the snapshots that expose the parts you'd like to forget. The apostle Paul, considered one of the great leaders in the New Testament, had a past he wished he could forget. His memory album was full of snapshots from his days of persecuting and killing Christians. What immense regret he could have been burdened with! But Paul understood that his past had been redeemed through God's healing and forgiveness.

How you view your past will affect how you live in the present and the future. Perhaps you have a past filled with regrets from actions that were wrong and hurtful. No matter what you've done, God is ready to forgive you, make you clean on the inside, and give you a fresh start—fully forgiven. Or perhaps you have a tragic past in which you were a victim of abuse, neglect, violence, or shameful acts. This is the most difficult past to deal with. But God wants to throw away all the bad snapshots and restore you like new—and he can if you'll let him. Regret, guilt, and shame can be removed, and you can be free to live in peace with godly purpose and abundant joy.

SHAME

How do I deal with my recurring feelings of shame?

PSALM 32:5 | *Finally, I confessed all my sins to you and stopped trying to hide my guilt. I said to myself, "I will confess my rebellion to the LORD." And you forgave me! All my guilt is gone.*

ISAIAH 54:4 | *Fear not; you will no longer live in shame. Don't be afraid; there is no more disgrace for you. You will no longer remember the shame of your youth.*

2 CORINTHIANS 5:17 | *Anyone who belongs to Christ has become a new person. The old life is gone; a new life has begun!*

TITUS 3:5 | *[God] saved us, not because of the righteous things we had done, but because of his mercy. He washed away our sins, giving us a new birth and new life through the Holy Spirit.*

Shame increases with unreleased guilt. God wants to release you from shame and restore you to a pure and holy relationship with himself. If your shame is the result of past sin, sincerely confess your sin to God and he will begin to take your shame away as you feel the freedom of his forgiveness.

When I've been humiliated, can I ever really recover?

JUDGES 16:21 | *The Philistines captured [Samson] and gouged out his eyes. They took him to Gaza, where he was bound with bronze chains and forced to grind grain in the prison.*

PSALM 51:3 | *I recognize my rebellion; it haunts me day and night.*

PSALM 119:5-6, 31, 39, 80 I *Oh, that my actions would consistently reflect your decrees! Then I will not be ashamed when I compare my life with your commands. . . . I cling to your laws. LORD, don't let me be put to shame! . . . Help me abandon my shameful ways; for your regulations are good. . . . May I be blameless in keeping your decrees; then I will never be ashamed.*

LUKE 22:60-62 I *Peter said, "Man, I don't know what you are talking about." And immediately, while he was still speaking, the rooster crowed. At that moment the Lord turned and looked at Peter. Suddenly, the Lord's words flashed through Peter's mind: "Before the rooster crows tomorrow morning, you will deny three times that you even know me." And Peter left the courtyard, weeping bitterly.*

Humiliation utterly destroys your self-respect and dignity. You can usually recover quickly from embarrassment—it often takes much longer to recover from humiliation and shame. No one likes to be humiliated, but it can be a watershed moment for spiritual repentance and restoration because it forces you to go to the only One who can offer complete forgiveness and restore your reputation. God promises to make you as clean as new-fallen snow and to turn your humiliation into an opportunity for him to show you his love, restore you, and raise you up again.

Sometimes your own actions cause you to be humiliated and feel shame, and sometimes you can be shamed by others. Samson and Peter felt deep shame and humiliation because of their sins. If you have experienced humiliation, especially if it was caused by your own sin, you may need to retreat for a while to demonstrate that your confession is real. But humiliation doesn't have to make you ineffective for God forever. He can and will restore you to full confidence and service if you allow him to do so.

SICKNESS/DAMAGED HEALTH

How do I find rest in times of poor health?

PSALM 38:3, 18, 22 I *Because of your anger, my whole body is sick; my health is broken because of my sins. . . . But I confess my sins; I am deeply sorry for what I have done. . . . Come quickly to help me, O Lord my savior.*

PSALM 119:93 I *I will never forget your commandments, for by them you give me life.*

Following God's direction can bring healing in your life. God's Word shows you how to break free from the stress, pressure, and unhealthy practices that undermine your health.

PSALM 73:24-26 I *You guide me with your counsel, leading me to a glorious destiny. Whom have I in heaven but you? I desire you more than anything on earth. My health may fail, and my spirit may grow weak, but God remains the strength of my heart; he is mine forever.*

Whether you have good health or poor health, you must rely on God for strength of spirit. Whether or not God chooses to heal you physically, you can have the unspeakable gift of knowing him personally and the comfort of walking with him daily. And he gives you the strength to hold on to your hope of eternal life, where there will be no more health problems.

PSALM 32:3-5 | *When I refused to confess my sin, my body wasted away, and I groaned all day long. Day and night your hand of discipline was heavy on me. My strength evaporated like water in the summer heat. Finally, I confessed all my sins to you and stopped trying to hide my guilt. I said to myself, "I will confess my rebellion to the LORD." And you forgave me! All my guilt is gone.*

Sin can make you sick, literally. Healing comes when you call on God for forgiveness. This takes the burden of guilt and shame off your back, and you will feel better, not only emotionally but physically as well.

Part Two

Questions for God

ACCEPTANCE

Am I really important to God?

GENESIS 1:26-27 | *God said, "Let us make human beings in our image, to be like us. They will reign over the fish in the sea, the birds in the sky, the livestock, all the wild animals on the earth, and the small animals that scurry along the ground." So God created human beings in his own image.*

PSALM 8:3-6 | *When I look at the night sky and see the work of your fingers . . . what are mere mortals that you should think about them, human beings that you should care for them? Yet you made them only a little lower than God and crowned them with glory and honor. You gave them charge of everything you made, putting all things under their authority.*

EPHESIANS 2:10 | *We are God's masterpiece. He has created us anew in Christ Jesus, so we can do the good things he planned for us long ago.*

God made you in his own image—you are his treasure and masterpiece! You are invaluable to him, which is why he sent his own Son to die for your sins so that you could live in heaven with him forever.

PSALM 139:13 | *You made all the delicate, inner parts of my body and knit me together in my mother's womb.*

JEREMIAH 1:5 | *I knew you before I formed you in your mother's womb. Before you were born I set you apart and appointed you as my prophet to the nations.*

God made you with great skill and crafted you with loving care. He showed how much value he places on you by the way he made you.

PSALM 139:17 | *How precious are your thoughts about me, O God. They cannot be numbered!*

Almighty God thinks wonderful thoughts about you all the time. He looks inside you and sees your real value.

PSALM 139:1-3 | *O LORD, you have examined my heart and know everything about me. You know when I sit down or stand up. You know my thoughts even when I'm far away. You see me when I travel and when I rest at home. You know everything I do.*

God values you so much that he watches over you no matter where you are or what you are doing. This tells you how special he thinks you are.

1 CORINTHIANS 6:19-20 | *Don't you realize that your body is the temple of the Holy Spirit, who lives in you and was given to you by God? You do not belong to yourself, for God bought you with a high price.*

God values you so much that he even allows your body to become the temple in which he lives. God does not need to live in you. He can live anywhere. But by choosing to live within you, he declares you his temple, his dwelling place. What a great value he places on you to do that!

GALATIANS 3:26 | *You are all children of God through faith in Christ Jesus.*

GALATIANS 4:7 | *You are no longer a slave but God's own child. And since you are his child, God has made you his heir.*

God values you so much that he thinks of you as his child.

MATTHEW 28:20 | *[Jesus said,] "Be sure of this: I am with you always, even to the end of the age."*

God's Son promises to be with you always. Why would he want to be with you if he didn't value you?

How does God show he cares for me?

PSALM 121:8 | *The LORD keeps watch over you as you come and go, both now and forever.*

PSALM 145:18-20 | *The LORD is close to all who call on him, yes, to all who call on him in truth. He grants the desires of those who fear him; he hears their cries for help and rescues them. The LORD protects all those who love him.*

MATTHEW 6:30 | *If God cares so wonderfully for wildflowers that are here today and thrown into the fire tomorrow, he will certainly care for you. Why do you have so little faith?*

1 PETER 5:7 | *Give all your worries and cares to God, for he cares about you.*

God is always close to you, ready to help in your time of need. His presence surrounds you, ready to protect you from Satan's attacks. God also sends blessings your way in a variety of forms: He sends opportunities your way, ready to make your life more full and satisfying. He promises that he is ready to take your worries and cares upon himself. And he offers you eternal life in heaven, away from all hurt, pain, and sin. He wants to do all these things for you—if you let him—because he cares about you.

Why does God show me mercy when my actions don't deserve it?

EXODUS 34:6 | *The LORD passed in front of Moses, calling out, . . . "The God of compassion and mercy! I am slow to anger and filled with unfailing love and faithfulness."*

MICAH 7:18 | *Where is another God like you, who pardons . . . guilt . . . , overlooking the sins of his special people? You will not stay angry with your people forever, because you delight in showing unfailing love.*

EPHESIANS 2:4-5 | *God is so rich in mercy, and he loved us so much, that even though we were dead because of our sins, he gave us life when he raised Christ from the dead.*

HEBREWS 4:16 | *Let us come boldly to the throne of our gracious God. There we will receive his mercy, and we will find grace to help us when we need it most.*

God's grace—his mercy—is undeserved favor. God shows you mercy because he loves you. He always will, thus he will always want to help you. Mercy is compassion poured out on needy people. Even when you don't deserve mercy, he still extends it to you. Your sin and rebellion against God deserve his punishment, but instead he offers you forgiveness and eternal life. And just as God is merciful toward you in spite of your sin, you should be able to extend mercy toward those who have wronged you.

How does God show me mercy?

PSALM 86:15 | *You, O Lord, are a God of compassion and mercy, slow to get angry and filled with unfailing love and faithfulness.*

God shows you mercy by being slow to get angry over your sins. He will show you unfailing love no matter what you have done against him.

How is God empathetic toward me?

ROMANS 8:34 | *Who then will condemn us? No one—for Christ Jesus died for us and was raised to life for us, and he is sitting in the place of honor at God's right hand, pleading for us.*

PHILIPPIANS 2:6-8 | *Though [Christ Jesus] was God, he did not think of equality with God as something to cling to. Instead, he gave up his divine privileges; he took the humble position of a slave and was born as a human being. When he appeared in human form, he humbled himself in obedience to God and died a criminal's death on a cross.*

COLOSSIANS 2:9 | *In Christ lives all the fullness of God in a human body.*

HEBREWS 5:2, 8 | *[Every high priest] is able to deal gently with ignorant and wayward people because he himself is subject to the same weaknesses. . . . Even though Jesus was God's Son, he learned obedience from the things he suffered.*

1 PETER 3:18 | *Christ suffered for our sins once for all time. He never sinned, but he died for sinners to bring you safely home to God. He suffered physical death, but he was raised to life in the Spirit.*

God not only created the entire range of human emotions but experienced them himself when he sent his Son, Jesus, to earth as a human being in order to fully experience the human condition. You can't say that God doesn't understand and feel your hurt and pain, for Jesus suffered great hurt and pain. Thus, his heart breaks when your heart breaks. He understands your weaknesses, your fears, and your joys. Instead of condemnation, he gives mercy; instead of criticism, he offers comfort and encouragement.

But even beyond that, his empathy and love for you moved him to create a way for you to experience *eternal* joy, free from all pain and suffering. However, he also gave you freedom of choice to accept his salvation because he understands that if he didn't give you that freedom, you would not be worshiping him of your own will.

FAULTS

With all my faults, how can God see me as blameless?

ROMANS 5:1 | *Since we have been made right in God's sight by faith, we have peace with God because of what Jesus Christ our Lord has done for us.*

1 CORINTHIANS 6:11 | *Some of you were once like that. But you were cleansed; you were made holy; you were made right with God by calling on the name of the Lord Jesus Christ and by the Spirit of our God.*

EPHESIANS 1:4 | *Even before he made the world, God loved us and chose us in Christ to be holy and without fault in his eyes.*

COLOSSIANS 1:22 | *[God] has reconciled you to himself through the death of Christ in his physical body. As a result, he has brought you into his own presence, and you are holy and blameless as you stand before him without a single fault.*

God sees you as blameless because of your belief and faith in Jesus' death on the cross in your place. Jesus took your sins away, so God sees you as though you had never sinned.

FORGIVENESS

What does it really mean to be forgiven by God?

ISAIAH 1:18 | *"Come now, let's settle this," says the LORD. "Though your sins are like scarlet, I will make them as white as snow. Though they are red like crimson, I will make them as white as wool."*

JEREMIAH 3:22 | *"My wayward children," says the LORD, "come back to me, and I will heal your wayward hearts." "Yes, we're coming," the people reply, "for you are the LORD our God."*

COLOSSIANS 1:22 | *You are holy and blameless as you stand before him without a single fault.*

Forgiveness means that God looks at you as though you had never sinned. When you receive his forgiveness, you become blameless before him. When God forgives, he doesn't sweep your sins under the carpet; instead, he completely washes them away. There is nothing like knowing that God has taken all your sins—the "little" sins and the horrible things you've done—and thrown them away. Experiencing the love and forgiveness of the almighty Creator after everything you've done is an amazing thing. It is one hundred times better than any feeling you can achieve from a substance or a habit. If you are sick of continuing to make the mistakes you do, accept what Jesus did for you and the healing and recovery he offers.

MATTHEW 5:44 | *Love your enemies! Pray for those who persecute you!*

Forgiveness paves the way for harmonious relationships, even with your enemies.

ROMANS 4:7 | *Oh, what joy for those whose disobedience is forgiven, whose sins are put out of sight.*

COLOSSIANS 2:13 | *You were dead because of your sins and because your sinful nature was not yet cut away. Then God made you alive with Christ, for he forgave all our sins.*

Forgiveness brings great joy because you have been freed from the heavy weight of guilt and because you no longer have to be a slave to your sinful nature.

ROMANS 10:9-10 | *If you confess with your mouth that Jesus is Lord and believe in your heart that God raised him from the dead, you will be saved. For it is by believing in your heart that you are made right with God, and it is by confessing with your mouth that you are saved.*

Receiving God's forgiveness is the only way you can have assurance of eternal life in heaven.

Can forgiveness of sin stop sin's consequences?

GENESIS 3:17 | *To the man [God] said, "Since you . . . ate from the tree whose fruit I commanded you not to eat, the ground is cursed because of you. All your life you will struggle to scratch a living from it."*

2 SAMUEL 12:13-14 | *David confessed to Nathan, "I have sinned against the LORD." Nathan replied, "Yes, but the LORD has forgiven you. . . . Nevertheless . . . your child will die."*

The consequences of sin are often irreversible. When God forgives you, he doesn't necessarily eliminate the results of your wrongdoing. He allows the natural effects of your actions to happen. This painful process should be a powerful reminder for you the next time you face temptation. The consequences are there for you to learn from your mistakes and become a stronger, wiser person.

I've done some pretty awful things. Is there a limit to how much God will forgive me?

EXODUS 34:7 | *I lavish unfailing love to a thousand generations. I forgive iniquity, rebellion, and sin.*

God's supply of forgiveness far exceeds the number of times you could ever go to him for forgiveness. He promises to forgive you whenever you humbly ask for it.

EZEKIEL 18:22 | *All their past sins will be forgotten, and they will live because of the righteous things they have done.*

MATTHEW 18:21-22 | *Peter . . . asked, "Lord, how often should I forgive someone who sins against me? Seven times?" "No, not seven times," Jesus replied, "but seventy times seven!"*

No matter how terrible your past or how many sins you have committed, if you approach God with an attitude of humble sincerity and confess your sins, he will forgive you. To think that some of your sins are "too bad" to be forgiven is to minimize the power of Jesus' death and resurrection on your behalf.

PSALM 51:11-12, 16-17 | *Do not banish me from your presence, and don't take your Holy Spirit from me. Restore to me the joy of your salvation, and make me willing to obey you. . . . You do not desire a sacrifice, or I would offer one. You do not want a burnt offering. The sacrifice you desire is a broken spirit. You will not reject a broken and repentant heart, O God.*

God's grace is greater than your failure. Temptation wins only when it keeps you from turning back to God. No matter how often you fail, God welcomes you back, and recovery begins when you return to God. He will not despise your broken and repentant heart—he promises to forgive you, help you start over, and give you joy.

FUTURE

What do I have to look forward to?

1 PETER 1:4-5 | *We have a priceless inheritance . . . that is kept in heaven for you, pure and undefiled, beyond the reach of change and decay. And through your faith, God is protecting you by his power until you receive this salvation, which is ready to be revealed on the last day for all to see.*

If you are a follower of Jesus, you have been adopted into God's family (see Ephesians 1:5), and as a child of God, you have an inheritance waiting for you in heaven that is beyond your imagination. Until you enter heaven, God preserves your inheritance there.

1 CORINTHIANS 2:9 | *No eye has seen, no ear has heard, and no mind has imagined what God has prepared for those who love him.*

Like most people, you probably don't think enough about the great future that awaits you beyond this mortal life. When you take time to ponder your glorious future, it puts everything in a new light.

1 CORINTHIANS 15:54-58 | *When our dying bodies have been transformed into bodies that will never die, this Scripture will be fulfilled: "Death is swallowed up in victory. O death, where is your victory? O death, where is your sting?" For sin is the sting that results in death, and the law gives sin its power. But thank God! He gives us victory over sin and death through our Lord Jesus Christ. So, my dear brothers and sisters, be strong and*

immovable. Always work enthusiastically for the Lord, for you know that nothing you do for the Lord is ever useless.

Once you have placed your trust in Jesus Christ, you need have no fear about death or about your future after death. Death is simply a doorway into your heavenly home. And this hope of eternal life gives you courage and discipline to live life well now, to live the way God says is best rather than the way that simply indulges your selfish desires.

GOD'S LOVE

How can I know God really loves me?

JOHN 3:16 | *God loved the world so much that he gave his one and only Son, so that everyone who believes in him will not perish but have eternal life.*

1 JOHN 3:1 | *See how very much our Father loves us, for he calls us his children.*

1 JOHN 4:9-10 | *God showed how much he loved us by sending his one and only Son into the world so that we might have eternal life through him. This is real love—not that we loved God, but that he loved us and sent his Son as a sacrifice to take away our sins.*

The gift of God's Son, Jesus Christ, is the ultimate expression of God's love for you. Though he gives many other blessings, he could give no greater gift.

ROMANS 5:5 | *We know how dearly God loves us, because he has given us the Holy Spirit to fill our hearts with his love.*

The gift of the Holy Spirit is also an assurance of God's love. Though the presence of the Holy Spirit may be difficult to prove objectively, the Spirit gives solid assurances in your heart.

ROMANS 8:38-39 | *Nothing can ever separate us from God's love. Neither death nor life, neither angels nor demons, neither our fears for today nor our worries about tomorrow—not even the powers of hell can separate us from God's love. No power in the sky above or in the earth below—indeed, nothing in all creation will ever be able to separate us from the love of God that is revealed in Christ Jesus our Lord.*

God promises that nothing can come between his love and you. Nothing!

What are the benefits of God's love for me?

PSALM 23:6 | *Surely your goodness and unfailing love will pursue me all the days of my life.*

You can be certain that God will continually shower you with his mercy and guard you with his love.

PSALM 31:7 | *I will be glad and rejoice in your unfailing love, for you have seen my troubles, and you care about the anguish of my soul.*

God understands your weaknesses and struggles, without condemning you.

PSALM 103:8 | *The LORD is compassionate and merciful, slow to get angry and filled with unfailing love.*

HEBREWS 13:5 | *God has said, "I will never fail you. I will never abandon you."*

While you, as a human being, may struggle to keep loving God, God never tires of nor gives up on loving you. He is not like you, subject to whims or moods or irritability or bad temper. You can trust that his love is, indeed, unfailing. He will never turn his back on you.

1 CORINTHIANS 2:9 | *No eye has seen, no ear has heard, and no mind has imagined what God has prepared for those who love him.*

You cannot imagine all that God has planned for you. Because he loves you, God is going to share his best with you for all eternity.

Why does God pursue me?

HOSEA 2:16, 23 | *"When that day comes," says the LORD . . . "I will show love to those I called 'Not loved.' And to those I called 'Not my people,' I will say, 'Now you are my people.' And they will reply, 'You are our God!'"*

1 THESSALONIANS 1:4 | *We know, dear brothers and sisters, that God loves you and has chosen you to be his own people.*

1 JOHN 3:1 | *See how very much our Father loves us, for he calls us his children, and that is what we are!*

God is looking for a personal relationship with each person he has created. He pursues you not to get something from you, but to give wonderful gifts to you: help, hope, power, salvation, joy, peace, and eternal life. No wonder he pursues you—he knows how much these gifts can transform your life forever. How long before he gets your attention?

HOPE

How do I put my hope in God?

ROMANS 8:24 | *We were given this hope when we were saved. (If we already have something, we don't need to hope for it.)*

Hope, by definition, is expecting something that has not yet occurred. Once hope is fulfilled, it isn't hope anymore. Thus, an important part of hope is waiting patiently for God to work.

HEBREWS 11:1 | *Faith is the confidence that what we hope for will actually happen; it gives us assurance about things we cannot see.*

You can choose to have faith in God to do what he has promised, trusting that he will. Your hopes are not idle hopes but are built on the solid foundation of his trustworthiness.

JEREMIAH 29:11 | *"I know the plans I have for you," says the LORD. "They are plans for good and not for disaster, to give you a future and a hope."*

PHILIPPIANS 3:13-14 | *Forgetting the past and looking forward to what lies ahead, I press on to reach the end of the race and receive the heavenly prize for which God, through Christ Jesus, is calling us.*

Hope involves an understanding of the future—that even here on earth God's plans are to bless you, not to hurt you. So if you follow his plans for you, you can look forward to your future with joyful anticipation.

MEANING

What brings meaning to my life? What will make my life count?

GENESIS 1:26 | *God said, "Let us make human beings in our image, to be like us. They will reign over the fish in the sea, the birds in the sky, the livestock, all the wild animals on the earth, and the small animals that scurry along the ground."*

ISAIAH 43:7 | *Bring all who claim me as their God, for I have made them for my glory. It was I who created them.*

ROMANS 11:36 | *Everything comes from [the Lord] and exists by his power and is intended for his glory.*

God, as your Creator, gives you value. You are made in his image, and his breath is the very reason you are alive.

ISAIAH 43:1 | *[The Lord says,] "I have called you by name; you are mine."*

EZEKIEL 29:21 | *They will know that I am the LORD.*

COLOSSIANS 3:10 | *Put on your new nature, and be renewed as you learn to know your Creator and become like him.*

You were created to know God and enjoy fellowship with him. What could be more meaningful than a relationship with God, your Creator?

PSALM 8:3-8 | *When I look at the night sky and see the work of your fingers—the moon and the stars you set in place—what are mere mortals that you should think about them, human beings that you should care for them? Yet you made them only a little lower than God and crowned them with glory and honor. You gave them charge of everything you made, putting all things under their authority—the flocks and the herds and all the wild animals, the birds in the sky, the fish in the sea, and everything that swims the ocean currents.*

God has given humans the highest place in creation and the great responsibility of managing and caring for his creation. This is a meaningful purpose and a high honor!

MATTHEW 4:19 | *Jesus called out . . . "Come, follow me, and I will show you how to fish for people!"*

2 CORINTHIANS 3:2 | *The only letter of recommendation we need is you yourselves. Your lives are a letter written in our hearts; everyone can read it and recognize our good work among you.*

You are called to participate in God's work in the world and to make an eternal impact on others for him.

JOHN 11:25-26 | *Jesus [said], "I am the resurrection and the life. Anyone who believes in me will live, even after dying. Everyone who lives in me and believes in me will never ever die. Do you believe this?"*

The fact that death is not the end for Jesus' followers infuses your life with eternal significance. Knowing there is life after death gives you true perspective on what you do here and now.

JOHN 6:27 | *Don't be so concerned about perishable things like food. Spend your energy seeking the eternal life that the Son of Man can give you.*

PHILIPPIANS 3:7-9 | *I once thought these things were valuable, but now I consider them worthless because of what Christ has done. Yes, everything else is worthless when compared with the infinite value of knowing Christ Jesus my Lord. For his sake I have discarded everything else, counting it all as garbage, so that I could gain Christ and become one with him.*

A personal, growing relationship with Jesus Christ today and throughout eternity gives life meaning. He created you for a purpose, and the better you know him, the clearer his purpose for you will become.

PSALM 40:8 | *I take joy in doing your will, my God, for your instructions are written on my heart.*

2 CORINTHIANS 5:9 | *Whether we are here in this body or away from this body, our goal is to please him.*

2 TIMOTHY 2:21 | *If you keep yourself pure, you will be a special utensil for honorable use. Your life will be clean, and you will be ready for the Master to use you for every good work.*

Pleasing God by obeying him and doing his will prepares you to be used by God to accomplish his purposes for your life.

MATTHEW 28:19-20 | *[Jesus said,] "Go and make disciples of all the nations, baptizing them in the name of the Father and the Son and the Holy Spirit. Teach these new disciples to obey all the commands I have given you. And be sure of this: I am with you always, even to the end of the age."*

ACTS 1:8 | *[Jesus said,] "You will receive power when the Holy Spirit comes upon you. And you will be my witnesses, telling people about me everywhere—in Jerusalem, throughout Judea, in Samaria, and to the ends of the earth."*

Of all the important work on earth, what could be more important than sharing God with others?

EPHESIANS 1:5 | *God decided in advance to adopt us into his own family by bringing us to himself through Jesus Christ. This is what he wanted to do, and it gave him great pleasure.*

God's purpose for you is to be one of his children and to live in the complete security of his love every moment.

OBEDIENCE

Obedience seems like such an authoritarian concept. Does God really require my total obedience?

DEUTERONOMY 6:18, 24-25 | *Do what is right and good in the LORD's sight, so all will go well with you. . . . The LORD our God commanded us to obey all these decrees and to fear him so he can continue to bless us and preserve our lives, as he has done to this day. For we will be counted as righteous when we obey all the commands the LORD our God has given us.*

JOHN 14:15 | *[Jesus said,] "If you love me, obey my commandments."*

1 JOHN 3:24 | *Those who obey God's commandments remain in fellowship with him, and he with them. And we know he lives in us because the Spirit he gave us lives in us.*

God's commandments are not burdensome obligations but pathways to joyful, meaningful, satisfying lives. And obeying God is the only way to stay in fellowship with him. God's call for your obedience is based on his own commitment to your well-being. Since God is the Creator of life, he knows how life is supposed to work. Obedience demonstrates your willingness to follow through on what he says, your trust that God's way is best for you, and your desire to have a close relationship with him.

How will God help me obey him?

PHILIPPIANS 2:12-13 | *Work hard to show the results of your salvation, obeying God with deep reverence and fear. For God is working in you, giving you the desire and the power to do what pleases him.*

When God requires something of you, he empowers you to do it. Not only does God guide you into the ways he has commanded, ways that are best for you, but he also gives you the power to live according to those ways.

JOHN 14:15-17 | *If you love me, obey my commandments. And I will ask the Father, and he will give you another Advocate, who will never leave you. He is the Holy Spirit, who leads into all truth. . . . You know him, because he lives with you now and later will be in you.*

The power God gives you is his own Holy Spirit, who is also called an Advocate. As your advocate, he comes alongside you not only to advise and inspire you but actually to live and work in you. Even as the air you breathe empowers your physical body, so the Holy Spirit empowers your obedience.

JAMES 1:25 | *If you look carefully into the perfect law that sets you free, and if you do what it says and don't forget what you heard, then God will bless you for doing it.*

Following God's Word sets you free from slavery to sin and all its ugly consequences so that you can be free to obey the Lord and enjoy all his wonderful blessings.

PRAYER

Does God always answer prayer?

PSALM 116:1-2 | *I love the LORD because he hears my voice and my prayer for mercy. Because he bends down to listen, I will pray as long as I have breath!*

1 PETER 3:12 | *The eyes of the Lord watch over those who do right, and his ears are open to their prayers. But the Lord turns his face against those who do evil.*

God listens carefully to every prayer and answers it. His answer may be yes, no, or wait. Any loving parent gives all three of these responses to a child. A yes answer to every request would spoil you and be dangerous to your well-being. Answering no to every request would be vindictive, stingy, and damaging to your spirit. Answering wait to every prayer would be frustrating. God always answers based on what he knows is best for you.

JAMES 5:16 | *The earnest prayer of a righteous person has great power and produces wonderful results.*

1 JOHN 5:14 | *We are confident that he hears us whenever we ask for anything that pleases him.*

As you maintain a close relationship with Jesus and consistently study his Word, your prayers will be more aligned with his will. When that happens, you are more apt to receive yes answers.

2 CORINTHIANS 12:8-9 | *Three different times [Paul] begged the Lord to take [the thorn in his flesh] away. Each time [the Lord] said, "My grace is all you need. My power works best in weakness."*

Sometimes, you will find that God answers prayer by giving you something better than you asked for. Or, as it was for Paul, the answer is what God deems best for you.

JOHN 11:3-6 | *The two sisters sent a message to Jesus telling him, "Lord, your dear friend is very sick." But when Jesus heard about it he said, "Lazarus's sickness will not end in death. No, it happened for the glory of God so that the Son of God will receive glory from this." So although Jesus loved Martha, Mary, and Lazarus, he stayed where he was for the next two days.*

God may be doing things behind the scenes, preparing you to experience him in greater ways than what you may be asking for. Mary and Martha didn't understand why Jesus didn't answer their prayer to come and heal their brother, Lazarus. Jesus waited because he had an answer better than anything they could imagine. When Jesus did come, their brother had been dead several days. But Jesus came to raise Lazarus from the dead to reveal his glory to many people and to strengthen their faith in him. Mary and Martha would have been grateful if God had simply healed Lazarus. But imagine their sheer joy at the sight of their brother alive again. Can you feel the excitement they must have felt watching their brother walk out to them? You, too, can have hope in times when God seems silent. God's answer will come.

PRESENCE OF GOD

Is God truly with me all the time?

PSALM 23:4 | *Even when I walk through the darkest valley, I will not be afraid, for you are close beside me.*

MATTHEW 28:20 | *[Jesus said,] "Be sure of this: I am with you always, even to the end of the age."*

God never promised that following him would free your life from trouble, but he does promise to be with you at all times and to help you work through your problems with more wisdom and less fear. Even in your darkest moments, when you need God most, he is ready and able to help when you ask him. Sometimes God can and does take away your problem. But many times God allows you to struggle through your problem so you can learn from it and grow stronger. Either way, he knows your trouble and walks beside you through it.

PSALM 18:6 | *In my distress I cried out to the LORD; yes, I prayed to my God for help. He heard me from his sanctuary; my cry to him reached his ears.*

PSALM 106:44 | *[The Lord] pitied [his people] in their distress and listened to their cries.*

JONAH 2:2 | *I cried out to the LORD in my great trouble, and he answered me. I called to you from the land of the dead, and LORD, you heard me!*

You need not pray for the Lord to be with you in times of crisis—he is already there. Instead, pray that you will recognize his presence and have the humility and discernment to accept his help.

Why do I sometimes feel that God is absent?

PSALM 10:1 | *O LORD, why do you stand so far away? Why do you hide when I am in trouble?*

PSALM 13:1-2 | *O LORD, how long will you forget me? Forever? How long will you look the other way? How long must I struggle with anguish in my soul, with sorrow in my heart every day? How long will my enemy have the upper hand?*

The greater your troubles, the further away God sometimes seems. Even faithful and godly King David, writer of many of the psalms, sometimes felt that God was absent. In your darkest hour, you may feel that God has left you. In times like this, when it seems as though God is absent, don't trust your feelings; trust God's promise that he will never leave you.

STRENGTH

How do I tap into God's strength to fight the battles of life?

JOSHUA 1:7-8 | *Be strong and very courageous. Be careful to obey all the instructions Moses gave you. Do not deviate from them, turning either to the right or to the left. Then you will be successful in everything you do. Study this Book of Instruction continually. Meditate on it day and night so you will be sure to obey everything written in it. Only then will you prosper and succeed in all you do.*

PSALM 119:9 | *How can a young person stay pure? By obeying your word.*

PSALM 119:105 | *Your word is a lamp to guide my feet and a light for my path.*

LUKE 11:28 | *Jesus replied, "But even more blessed are all who hear the word of God and put it into practice."*

God's Word, the Bible, is your secret weapon in fighting the battles of life because in it you find the battle strategy as outlined by God Almighty himself. God, the Creator of life, tells you how to live life to the fullest. But if you don't study God's Word, you will miss the strategies that will help you overcome anything life throws at you.

1 TIMOTHY 6:12 | *Fight the good fight for the true faith. Hold tightly to the eternal life to which God has called you, which you have confessed so well before many witnesses.*

2 TIMOTHY 4:7 | *I have fought the good fight, I have finished the race, and I have remained faithful.*

2 TIMOTHY 4:18 | *The Lord will deliver me . . . safely into his heavenly Kingdom.*

Always keep your eyes on the end goal, which is heaven. In this life you will face struggles, hardships, and spiritual battles. But if you make each decision as an investment in eternity, your life will make sense and have purpose and direction.

1 CORINTHIANS 1:8-9 | *He will keep you strong to the end so that you will be free from all blame on the day when our Lord Jesus*

Christ returns. God will do this, for he is faithful to do what he says, and he has invited you into partnership with his Son, Jesus Christ our Lord.

EPHESIANS 3:16 | *I pray that from his glorious, unlimited resources he will empower you with inner strength through his Spirit.*

PHILIPPIANS 4:13 | *I can do everything through Christ, who gives me strength.*

2 THESSALONIANS 3:3 | *The Lord is faithful; he will strengthen you and guard you from the evil one.*

Don't underestimate the strength that God has promised to provide if you just ask him. Claim God's promises, walk in his presence, accept his protection, and you will be strong enough to face any foe.

ROMANS 1:11 | *I long to visit you so I can bring you some spiritual gift that will help you grow strong in the Lord.*

PHILIPPIANS 1:27-28 | *You must live as citizens of heaven, conducting yourselves in a manner worthy of the Good News about Christ. Then . . . you are standing together with one spirit and one purpose, fighting together for the faith, which is the Good News. Don't be intimidated in any way by your enemies.*

1 THESSALONIANS 3:2-3 | *We sent Timothy to visit you . . . to strengthen you, to encourage you in your faith, and to keep you from being shaken by the troubles you were going through.*

Stand together with other Christians. Wars are not fought and won with one soldier.

TRUSTING GOD

What makes God trustworthy?

TITUS 1:2 | *[The] truth gives [those whom God has chosen] confidence that they have eternal life, which God—who does not lie—promised them before the world began.*

You can trust God because he never lies. In fact, he *is* truth—he is the source of truth and all truth flows from him. Therefore, he is completely trustworthy, and knowing his truths frees you from the ignorance and deception of what the world claims is true.

JOHN 3:16 | *God loved the world so much that he gave his one and only Son, so that everyone who believes in him will not perish but have eternal life.*

You can trust God because he loves you and therefore always has your best interests at heart.

MALACHI 3:6 | *I am the LORD, and I do not change.*

HEBREWS 1:10-12 | *In the beginning, Lord, you laid the foundation of the earth and made the heavens with your hands. They will perish, but you remain forever. They will wear out like old clothing. . . . But you are always the same; you will live forever.*

HEBREWS 13:8 | *Jesus Christ is the same yesterday, today, and forever.*

You can trust God because he is eternally unchanging. You never have to worry whether his character or attitude toward you will be different tomorrow.

PSALM 19:7 I *The instructions of the LORD are perfect, reviving the soul. The decrees of the LORD are trustworthy, making wise the simple.*

PSALM 111:7 I *All he does is just and good, and all his commandments are trustworthy.*

PROVERBS 30:5 I *Every word of God proves true. He is a shield to all who come to him for protection.*

You can trust God because everything he says and does is just and good.

PSALM 16:10 I *You will not leave my soul among the dead or allow your holy one to rot in the grave.*

PSALM 22:16, 18 I *My enemies surround me like a pack of dogs; an evil gang closes in on me. They have pierced my hands and feet. . . . They divide my garments among themselves and throw dice for my clothing.*

JOHN 12:44 I *Jesus shouted to the crowds, "If you trust me, you are trusting not only me, but also God who sent me."*

2 CORINTHIANS 1:20 I *All of God's promises have been fulfilled in Christ with a resounding "Yes!"*

1 PETER 1:21 I *Through Christ you have come to trust in God. And you have placed your faith and hope in God because he raised Christ from the dead and gave him great glory.*

We know that all Jesus' promises about his death and resurrection came true, so we know we can trust what Jesus said. You can trust that all God's promises will come true, as well, for God's promises about the death and resurrection of a Savior came long before Jesus was born, and they came true.

PSALM 40:2-3 | *[The Lord] lifted me out of the pit of despair, out of the mud and the mire. He set my feet on solid ground and steadied me as I walked along. He has given me a new song to sing, a hymn of praise to our God. Many will see what he has done and be amazed. They will put their trust in the LORD.*

2 CORINTHIANS 3:18 | *All of us who have had that veil removed can see and reflect the glory of the Lord. And the Lord—who is the Spirit—makes us more and more like him as we are changed into his glorious image.*

COLOSSIANS 1:6 | *This same Good News that came to you is going out all over the world. It is bearing fruit everywhere by changing lives, just as it changed your lives from the day you first heard and understood the truth about God's wonderful grace.*

God's power and strength have been demonstrated in many lives of those around you. The undeniable facts of changed lives should give you confidence that you can trust who God is and what he can accomplish.

Part Three

The Twelve Steps to Recovery

STEP 1

"We admitted that we were powerless over our dependencies—that our lives had become unmanageable."*

What is the significance of admitting that I cannot control my actions?

ROMANS 7:18 | *I know that nothing good lives in me, that is, in my sinful nature. I want to do what is right, but I can't.*

ROMANS 7:21 | *I have discovered this principle of life—that when I want to do what is right, I inevitably do what is wrong.*

2 CORINTHIANS 3:5 | *It is not that we think we are qualified to do anything on our own. Our qualification comes from God.*

Admitting that you are powerless over the things you struggle with can be a hard thing to do. However, insisting that you can control your addictions has put you where you are today, and your situation will only get worse if you don't do something—your dependencies will continue to control your life until everything you value is gone. The

---

*These twelve steps are as published by Alcoholics Anonymous. See www.
alcoholicsanonymous.ie/opencontent/default.asp?itemid=10&section=12+Steps+
%2D+12+Traditions.

earlier you admit your problem—no matter how far along it has taken you—the better off you will be. Although there is no instant cure to your problem, admitting your powerlessness over it and God's ability to help is the first step toward your recovery.

What can I do when I feel helpless?

PSALM 30:10 | *Hear me, LORD, and have mercy on me. Help me, O LORD.*

PSALM 39:12 | *Hear my prayer, O LORD! Listen to my cries for help! Don't ignore my tears.*

Honestly tell God how you feel, and then don't be too proud to ask for his help. When you ask God for his help, you are acknowledging your need of him and of his ability to help you.

GENESIS 18:14 | *Is anything too hard for the LORD?*

2 CHRONICLES 14:11 | *Asa cried out to the LORD his God, "O LORD, no one but you can help the powerless. . . . It is in your name that we have come."*

PSALM 28:7 | *The LORD is my strength and shield. I trust him with all my heart. He helps me, and my heart is filled with joy. I burst out in songs of thanksgiving.*

When you ask God for help and trust that he will help, you open the lifeline to the God who loves doing the impossible! If you focus on trying to get yourself out of trouble, you may never see what God can do.

PSALM 138:3 | *As soon as I pray, you answer me; you encourage me by giving me strength.*

PHILIPPIANS 4:13 | *I can do everything through Christ, who gives me strength.*

You need God's strength to do what you can't do on your own.

STEP 2

"We came to believe that a Power greater than ourselves could restore us to sanity."

Why should I have confidence in God's ability and desire to help me?

PSALM 135:5 | *I know the greatness of the LORD—that our Lord is greater than any other god.*

2 CORINTHIANS 5:15 | *[Christ] died for everyone so that those who receive his new life will no longer live for themselves. Instead, they will live for Christ, who died and was raised for them.*

1 JOHN 4:4 | *You belong to God, my dear children. You have already won a victory over those people, because the Spirit who lives in you is greater than the spirit who lives in the world.*

God loves you so much that he sent his Son, Jesus, to die for you and rise from the dead so that you could live a transformed life now and enjoy life in heaven forever. This alone should give you great confidence that, more than anything, he wants to help you become all he created you to be.

EPHESIANS 6:16 | *Hold up the shield of faith to stop the fiery arrows of the devil.*

Your faith in God is like a shield that blocks the temptations and criticisms hurled at you every day. Without faith, your shield hangs uselessly at your side, and the arrows shot at you by your enemies pierce and defeat you. So even when life seems overwhelming, hold tightly to your faith. Raise it like a shield, and you will withstand the dangers and discouragements sent at you. And rejoice, knowing that God has already won the victory that can transform you now and forever.

How do I fill the emptiness inside me?

EPHESIANS 3:19 | *May you experience the love of Christ, though it is too great to understand fully. Then you will be made complete with all the fullness of life and power that comes from God.*

TITUS 3:5-6 | *[God] saved us, not because of the righteous things we had done, but because of his mercy. He washed away our sins, giving us a new birth and new life through the Holy Spirit. He generously poured out the Spirit upon us through Jesus Christ our Savior.*

God promises you the gift of his presence. When you accept this gift, God himself breaks into the empty chambers of your heart. His presence goes with you, along with his love, help, encouragement, peace, and comfort. If you are not filled with God's presence, your heart is like an empty home, waiting to be occupied by someone or something else that can never fulfill you.

JOHN 4:13-14 | *Jesus [said], "Anyone who drinks this water will soon become thirsty again. But those who drink the water I give will never be thirsty again. It becomes a fresh, bubbling spring within them, giving them eternal life."*

JOHN 10:10 | *The thief's purpose is to steal and kill and destroy. My purpose is to give them a rich and satisfying life.*

The inevitability of death can make life seem meaningless if you believe there is nothing beyond it. But if you are in a relationship with Jesus, you will experience life to its fullest and you will receive blessings here on earth and the promise of eternal life with him. This doesn't mean that you won't go through trials here on earth. Hard times are inevitable. But these hard times will not stop you from experiencing a fulfilling life, especially when you realize that this life is to prepare you for the next one, in heaven. How can you prepare yourself for the next life? By discovering your meaning and purpose in this life.

Where can I find real meaning and purpose in life?

PSALM 40:8 | *I take joy in doing your will, my God, for your instructions are written on my heart.*

JEREMIAH 29:11 | *"I know the plans I have for you," says the LORD. "They are plans for good and not for disaster, to give you a future and a hope."*

Meaning in life comes from obeying God and doing his will—both his will for all believers, which is found in the Bible, and his will for you personally, which is discovered through prayer and a relationship with him. The ultimate aim in life is to reach the goals God wants for you, not to reach the ones you want. Once you start moving toward the goals God has planned for you, you will realize that these are the ones you want to achieve as well, because you will find yourself happy and fulfilled.

MATTHEW 4:19 | *Jesus called out . . . "Come, follow me, and I will show you how to fish for people!"*

MATTHEW 28:18-20 | *Jesus [said], "I have been given all authority in heaven and on earth. Therefore, go and make disciples of all the nations, baptizing them in the name of the Father and the Son and the Holy Spirit. Teach these new disciples to obey all the commands I have given you. And be sure of this: I am with you always, even to the end of the age."*

ACTS 20:24 | *My life is worth nothing to me unless I use it for finishing the work assigned me by the Lord Jesus—the work of telling others the Good News about the wonderful grace of God.*

The plan God holds for all believers is to fulfill the great commission, which is to tell others about Jesus, thus building the Kingdom of God. This is something that you can and will want to do when you have seen how God has helped you recover.

JEREMIAH 1:5 | *I knew you before I formed you in your mother's womb. Before you were born I set you apart and appointed you.*

ROMANS 12:4-6 | *Just as our bodies have many parts and each part has a special function, so it is with Christ's body. We are many parts of one body, and we all belong to each other. In his grace, God has given us different gifts for doing certain things well.*

EPHESIANS 2:10 | *We are God's masterpiece. He has created us anew in Christ Jesus, so we can do the good things he planned for us long ago.*

1 TIMOTHY 4:14-15 | *Do not neglect the spiritual gift you received. . . . Give your complete attention to these matters. Throw yourself into your tasks so that everyone will see your progress.*

The plan that God holds for you personally is special and particular to you. Realize that God made you specifically for a purpose. God knows your desires and passions, and he knows that his will for you (the path he wants you to take in life) will be the most fulfilling one that you can possibly imagine. Do you want to live a life of meaning and passion? Discover this personal plan that God has for you.

MATTHEW 25:23 | *The master said, "Well done, my good and faithful servant."*

You have the opportunity to live in such a way that you will receive Jesus' words of commendation at the end of your life on this earth. How awesome it will be when you get to heaven and the God of the universe tells you, "Well done!"

Why does life sometimes seem so empty?

1 SAMUEL 12:21 | *Don't go back to worshiping worthless idols that cannot help or rescue you—they are totally useless!*

MICAH 6:14 | *You will eat but never have enough. Your hunger pangs and emptiness will remain. And though you try to save your money, it will come to nothing in the end.*

Remember when you were a child and you got something you wanted? When you grew tired of it after a while, you wanted something different to make you happy, right? This is exactly how sin works. Rather than feeling constantly empty from chasing sin, try feeling constantly fulfilled by doing what God wants you to do. This feeling is nothing less than amazing.

PROVERBS 21:17 | *Those who love pleasure become poor; those who love wine and luxury will never be rich.*

PROVERBS 27:20 | *Just as Death and Destruction are never satisfied, so human desire is never satisfied.*

ECCLESIASTES 2:1-3, 25 | *I said to myself, "Come on, let's try pleasure. Let's look for the 'good things' in life." But I found that this, too, was meaningless. So I said, "Laughter is silly. What good does it do to seek pleasure?" After much thought, I decided to cheer myself with wine. And while still seeking wisdom, I clutched at foolishness. In this way, I tried to experience the only happiness most people find during their brief life in this world. . . . For who can eat or enjoy anything apart from [God]?*

Feelings of emptiness come when seeking pleasure is your top priority. Pleasure feels good, but for only a short time. The more you seek pleasure, the more frequently you need it to satisfy. The satisfaction lasts only until you need your next fix of it, so you are caught in a meaningless cycle. However, the pleasure that God gives you (if you put your trust in him instead of in things) lasts forever. It gives a feeling that is far better than the feelings that worldly pleasures can give to you.

The reason this step is put into the twelve-step program is because of the countless lives God has changed. These changes are not based on feelings, although they change for the better as well, but on lives completely turned around and made whole.

ISAIAH 41:29 | *[Your idols] are all foolish, worthless things. All your idols are as empty as the wind.*

ISAIAH 44:10, 17-18 | *Who but a fool would make his own god—an idol that cannot help him one bit? . . . He falls down in front of it, worshiping and praying to it. "Rescue me!" he says. "You are my god!" Such stupidity and ignorance! Their eyes are closed, and they cannot see. Their minds are shut, and they cannot think.*

ISAIAH 46:7 | *[Some people] carry [a god] around on their shoulders, and when they set it down, it stays there. It can't even move! And when someone prays to it, there is no answer. It can't rescue anyone from trouble.*

God created you to have a relationship with him. He created that need in you. When you push the Creator into a corner of your heart or push him out entirely, you leave a big, empty hole. A heart without God is an empty heart.

How does God restore me?

ISAIAH 1:18 | *"Come now, let's settle this," says the LORD. "Though your sins are like scarlet, I will make them as white as snow. Though they are red like crimson, I will make them as white as wool."*

JEREMIAH 3:22 | *"My wayward children," says the LORD, "come back to me, and I will heal your wayward hearts." "Yes, we're coming," the people reply, "for you are the LORD our God."*

COLOSSIANS 1:22 | *[God] has reconciled you to himself through the death of Christ in his physical body. As a result, he has brought you into his own presence, and you are holy and blameless as you stand before him without a single fault.*

1 JOHN 1:9 | *If we confess our sins to him, he is faithful and just to forgive us our sins and to cleanse us.*

God forgives your mistakes and your sins if you ask him. After he forgives you, he looks at you as though you had never sinned. A holy and pure God cannot live in the presence of the contamination of sin, so you must be washed clean of the stain sin leaves in you before you can live in his presence. Forgiveness scrubs away the sin and its stain so you can be restored to purity in God's eyes.

PSALM 51:12 | *Restore to me the joy of your salvation, and make me willing to obey you.*

LAMENTATIONS 5:21 | *Restore us, O LORD, and bring us back to you again! Give us back the joys we once had!*

EZEKIEL 36:26-27 | *[The sovereign Lord said,] "I will give you a new heart, and I will put a new spirit in you. I will take out your stony, stubborn heart and give you a tender, responsive heart. And I will put my Spirit in you so that you will follow my decrees and be careful to obey my regulations."*

2 CORINTHIANS 5:17 | *Anyone who belongs to Christ has become a new person. The old life is gone; a new life has begun!*

God makes you new! He re-creates you so you can live in full fellowship with him, joyfully wanting to be like him.

PSALM 23:3 | *[The Lord] renews my strength. He guides me along right paths, bringing honor to his name.*

ISAIAH 40:31 | *Those who trust in the LORD will find new strength. They will soar high on wings like eagles. They will run and not grow weary. They will walk and not faint.*

When you put your faith in God, he restores your strength.

EPHESIANS 4:21-24 | *Since you have heard about Jesus and have learned the truth that comes from him, throw off your . . . former way of life. . . . Instead, let the Spirit renew your thoughts and attitudes. Put on your new nature, created to be like God—truly righteous and holy.*

COLOSSIANS 3:10 | *Put on your new nature, and be renewed as you learn to know your Creator and become like him.*

When you let the Holy Spirit control you, he restores your mind to so you can dwell more on what is good than on what is bad.

PSALM 34:18 | *The LORD is close to the brokenhearted; he rescues those whose spirits are crushed.*

When you come into his presence, God restores you emotionally, healing your hurts.

STEP 3

"We made a decision to turn our wills and our lives over to the care of God."

What difference will it make for me today if I place my full assurance in God?

PSALM 32:8 | *The LORD says, "I will guide you along the best pathway for your life. I will advise you and watch over you."*

PHILIPPIANS 1:6 | *God, who began the good work within you, will continue his work until it is finally finished on the day when Christ Jesus returns.*

Most likely, you sometimes doubt God's care. You are tempted to think he is not paying attention to you or is giving you only the bare minimum. But God, your loving Father, will always give you his best—you must cling to this hope. You should not allow the limitations of your finite perspective to blind you to the promise that God loves you and will complete his work in you.

ROMANS 5:3-5 | *We can rejoice, too, when we run into problems and trials, for we know that they help us develop endurance. And endurance develops strength of character, and character strengthens our confident hope of salvation. And this hope will not lead to disappointment. For we know how dearly God loves us, because he has given us the Holy Spirit to fill our hearts with his love.*

This world is God's waiting room. While you wait, you learn how to live and trust. You gain composure, strength, humility, and a deepening appreciation for God's care in your life.

PSALM 3:5 | *I lay down and slept, yet I woke up in safety, for the LORD was watching over me.*

ISAIAH 43:1-2 | *Listen to the LORD who created you. . . . The one who formed you says, "Do not be afraid, for I have ransomed you. I have called you by name; you are mine. When you go through deep waters, I will be with you. When you go through rivers of difficulty, you will not drown. When you walk through the fire of oppression, you will not be burned up; the flames will not consume you."*

ROMANS 15:13 | *I pray that God, the source of hope, will fill you completely with joy and peace because you trust in him. Then you will overflow with confident hope through the power of the Holy Spirit.*

The Bible provides example after example that placing your assurance in God gives you inner peace regardless of life's circumstances. This helps you focus on the process of recovery, not on the things that worry you.

How can I make peace with God so I can recover?

ROMANS 2:10 | *There will be glory and honor and peace from God for all who do good.*

Peace with God comes from establishing a relationship with him and then living the way he created you to live. This happens as you develop a closer relationship with your Creator. Then it becomes easier to see how his standards for living bring real peace, joy, and freedom from whatever is trying to enslave you.

PSALM 25:9 | *[The Lord] leads the humble in doing right, teaching them his way.*

MATTHEW 18:4 | *Anyone who becomes as humble as this little child is the greatest in the Kingdom of Heaven.*

1 PETER 5:6 | *Humble yourselves under the mighty power of God, and at the right time he will lift you up in honor.*

Humility before God brings peace because God blesses the humble. When you are humble, you understand your place in relation to God and others. Humility gives you a realistic view of yourself. This realization will open your eyes and motivate you to recover.

PHILIPPIANS 4:6-7 | *Don't worry about anything; instead, pray about everything. Tell God what you need, and thank him for all he has done. Then you will experience God's peace, which exceeds anything we can understand. His peace will guard your hearts and minds as you live in Christ Jesus.*

Pray about everything. You will discover peace when you accept that God wants to be included in every part of your day. He really will help if you ask him.

What is obedience to God? Why is it important?

JEREMIAH 7:23 | *Obey me, and I will be your God, and you will be my people. Do everything as I say, and all will be well!*

Obedience is defined as "being submissive to an authority." Ironically, obedience to God's ways actually frees you to enjoy life as he originally created it, keeping you from becoming entangled or enslaved to the sinful things that distract or hurt you. It protects you from the evil that God knows is out there, leads you on right paths where you will find blessing, and directs you into service that will please him and leave you fulfilled.

How can I experience God's presence in my life?

JOHN 14:6 | *Jesus [said], "I am the way, the truth, and the life. No one can come to the Father except through me."*

EPHESIANS 2:18 | *All of us can come to the Father through the same Holy Spirit because of what Christ has done for us.*

EPHESIANS 3:12 | *Because of Christ and our faith in him, we can now come boldly and confidently into God's presence.*

COLOSSIANS 1:22 | *[God] has reconciled you to himself through the death of Christ in his physical body. As a result, he has brought you into his own presence, and you are holy and blameless as you stand before him without a single fault.*

HEBREWS 10:19-22 | *We can boldly enter heaven's Most Holy Place because of the blood of Jesus. By his death, Jesus opened a new and life-giving way through the curtain into the Most Holy Place. And since we have a great High Priest who rules over God's house, let us go right into the presence of God with sincere hearts fully trusting him. For our guilty consciences have been sprinkled with Christ's blood to make us clean, and our bodies have been washed with pure water.*

A holy God cannot be in the presence of sin, so how can a sinful person experience God's presence? It is because of your faith in Jesus Christ's life, death, and resurrection. He died and took the punishment for your sins. If you've asked Jesus to forgive your sins, as far as God is concerned you now stand holy and blameless in his presence. He sees you as if you've never sinned, and he welcomes you into his presence, into a relationship with him, and into the one true way to get rid of all the things that control you and leave you unfulfilled.

PSALM 145:18 | *The LORD is close to all who call on him, yes, to all who call on him in truth.*

The Lord invites you to call on him without hesitation. He promises to reveal himself to you if your heart is sincere in wanting to know him—not just wanting to use him to make your life better. If it is hard to want to know him, put yourself in the position of a parent. Wouldn't you (or don't you) want to really know your child, since he or she is probably a lot like you? God created you to be a lot like he is so that your relationship with him could be satisfying. Hopefully it will spark your curiosity to know that the Creator of the universe and the Master of relationships wants to bond with you. This bond is as real as—and far more fulfilling than—any other relationship.

How can my heart become more like God wants it to be?

EZEKIEL 36:26 | *[The sovereign Lord said,] "I will give you a new heart, and I will put a new spirit in you. I will take out your stony, stubborn heart and give you a tender, responsive heart."*

You must desire a change of heart, and then God will help. It is hard to get rid of the sins that control your mind until your heart has started to change.

EZRA 1:5 | *God stirred the hearts of the priests and Levites and the leaders . . . to go to Jerusalem to rebuild the Temple of the LORD.*

God stirs your heart with right desires. It is then up to you to act upon them.

How can I become stronger in my faith, trusting God to care for me?

ROMANS 5:3-4 | *We can rejoice, too, when we run into problems and trials, for we know that they help us develop endurance.*

*And endurance develops strength of character, and character
strengthens our confident hope of salvation.*

2 CORINTHIANS 12:10 | *I take pleasure in my weaknesses, and in
the insults, hardships, persecutions, and troubles that I suffer
for Christ. For when I am weak, then I am strong.*

JAMES 1:2-4 | *When troubles come your way, consider it an
opportunity for great joy. For you know that when your faith
is tested, your endurance has a chance to grow. So let it grow,
for when your endurance is fully developed, you will be perfect
and complete, needing nothing.*

1 PETER 1:6-7 | *Be truly glad. There is wonderful joy ahead,
even though you have to endure many trials for a little while.
These trials will show that your faith is genuine. It is being
tested as fire tests and purifies gold—though your faith is far
more precious than mere gold. So when your faith remains
strong through many trials, it will bring you much praise and
glory and honor on the day when Jesus Christ is revealed to
the whole world.*

There must be something to the many verses that mention
how one's faith is strengthened through trials and trouble,
for the Bible wouldn't contain these verses if the writers
didn't know it was true. How did these writers know that
faith is strengthened through hard times? Because they
went through hard times themselves and had their faith in
God strengthened because God helped them! Know that
God will help you in your recovery. Then at the end, you
will be strong in your faith because you will truly know
that God really does help you through hard times.

STEP 4

"We made a searching and fearless moral inventory of ourselves."

How do I know what is right and true? How do I take a moral inventory?

PSALM 33:4 | *The word of the LORD holds true, and we can trust everything he does.*

PSALM 119:91 | *Your regulations remain true to this day, for everything serves your plans.*

PSALM 119:160 | *The very essence of your words is truth; all your just regulations will stand forever.*

PROVERBS 30:5 | *Every word of God proves true.*

ISAIAH 40:8 | *The grass withers, and the flowers fade, but the word of our God stands forever.*

JOHN 3:33 | *Anyone who accepts his testimony can affirm that God is true.*

ROMANS 3:4 | *Even if everyone else is a liar, God is true. As the Scriptures say about him, "You will be proved right in what you say, and you will win your case in court."*

Nothing impacts your daily life as much as the concept of truth. Discovering what is real is the only way to begin taking your moral inventory. Only then do you have a standard by which to evaluate your life. First, there's "telling the truth." People gravitate toward those who tell the truth because they are honest and can be trusted. Without trust, relationships fall apart. Second, there's absolute truth—fundamental principles of nature, science, and human behavior that were built into the universe from the beginning of time. For example, the truth (or law) of gravity is that when you drop an object it will fall. A truth of mathematics is that two plus two equals four. A truth of biology is that the right amounts of hydrogen and oxygen make water. A truth about life in general is that every person enters this world as a baby and someday exits this world through death. Only a fool would argue that these aren't true. There is nothing any person can do to change these fundamental truths about how the world works.

The Bible claims there is a third kind of truth— spiritual truth, moral and supernatural principles about human relationships with God and others that are absolute and constant in spite of people's feelings and beliefs to the contrary. Human beings have always wanted to reserve the right to determine this kind of truth for themselves or to believe that this kind of truth doesn't exist at all. Ironically, it's this kind of truth that, while more difficult to discover, will most affect the way you live both here on earth and where you spend eternity. Just as you can't reject the truth about gravity and expect to function well in this world, you can't ignore or reject truth about God and how he has determined human life should work. It's wise to discover and study this kind of truth because it so completely impacts the life of every human being on the planet. You are free to ignore spiritual truth if you so choose, but you do so at your own risk, now and for eternity.

How does seeking truth impact my relationship with God?

PSALM 9:10 | *Those who know your name trust in you, for you, O LORD, do not abandon those who search for you.*

PSALM 89:2 | *Your unfailing love will last forever. Your faithfulness is as enduring as the heavens.*

TITUS 1:2 | *This truth gives them confidence that they have eternal life, which God—who does not lie—promised them before the world began.*

Because God is utterly trustworthy, you can depend on what he says because he always tells the truth. Nothing he has said in his Word, the Bible, has ever been proven wrong or false. He specifically created you in order to have a relationship with you for all eternity. If God says he loves you—and he always tells the truth—you can be sure he desires a relationship with you.

How does my conscience work?

ROMANS 1:19-21 | *They know the truth about God because he has made it obvious to them. For ever since the world was created, people have seen the earth and sky. Through everything God made, they can clearly see his invisible qualities—his eternal power and divine nature. So they have no excuse for not knowing God. Yes, they knew God, but they wouldn't worship him as God or even give him thanks. And they began to think up foolish ideas of what God was like. As a result, their minds became dark and confused.*

1 TIMOTHY 1:19 | *Cling to your faith in Christ, and keep your conscience clear. For some people have deliberately violated their consciences; as a result, their faith has been shipwrecked.*

Conscience is the innate part of you that tells you whether or not you are in line with God's way of living. It is God's gift to you to keep you sensitive to his moral code. But you must use the gift. If you don't listen to and obey your conscience, it will become dull, and you will have a hard time hearing it. In addition, it will malfunction if not properly used. Your conscience will function effectively only when you stay close to God, spend time in his Word, and make an effort to understand yourself and your own personal tendencies of doing what is wrong. If your conscience is working faithfully, it will activate your heart and mind to know what is right and what is wrong. You will have a strong inner sense, a voice of accountability, to do what is right. If you have a reputation for not always doing the right thing or if you find yourself unmoved by evil, it may be an indication that your conscience has become dull or inactive. Let God, through his holy Word, sharpen and resensitize your conscience. Then it will speak to you in concert with God himself.

What should I avoid?

1 THESSALONIANS 5:22 | *Stay away from every kind of evil.*

1 PETER 2:11 | *Keep away from worldly desires that wage war against your very souls.*

As much as you possibly can, avoid sin and anything that will lead you into sin.

1 CORINTHIANS 10:14 | *Flee from the worship of idols.*

1 JOHN 5:21 | *Keep away from anything that might take God's place in your hearts.*

Avoid allowing anything or anyone to become more important to you than God.

PROVERBS 4:24 | *Avoid all perverse talk; stay away from corrupt speech.*

PROVERBS 20:3 | *Avoiding a fight is a mark of honor; only fools insist on quarreling.*

PHILIPPIANS 2:14 | *Do everything without complaining and arguing.*

2 TIMOTHY 2:16 | *Avoid worthless, foolish talk that only leads to more godless behavior.*

Avoid gossiping; complaining; quarreling; or saying things that are perverse, foul, or hurtful to others.

How can I develop stronger convictions about deciding to do the right thing?

PROVERBS 2:8-9 | *[The Lord] guards the paths of the just and protects those who are faithful to him. Then you will understand what is right, just, and fair, and you will find the right way to go.*

GALATIANS 5:16-17 | *Let the Holy Spirit guide your lives. Then you won't be doing what your sinful nature craves. The sinful nature wants to do evil, which is just the opposite of what the Spirit wants. And the Spirit gives us desires that are the opposite of what the sinful nature desires. These two forces are constantly fighting each other, so you are not free to carry out your good intentions.*

Every day you are faced with opportunities to choose right from wrong, good from bad, God's way or the way of the world. It takes practice to consistently choose God's way. It doesn't just happen all at once. But be tenacious in your commitment to not let Satan take over any more territory in your heart. Be committed to winning even the little battles so that your heart will eventually be fully devoted to God.

ISAIAH 51:7 | *Listen to me, you who know right from wrong, you who cherish my law in your hearts. Do not be afraid of people's scorn, nor fear their insults.*

Be committed to studying God's Word so that you can obey it. Do not be intimidated when others make fun of you for living by the principles of Scripture. Your convictions will be rewarded by God.

PSALM 37:30 | *The godly offer good counsel; they teach right from wrong.*

Get advice from godly people who have demonstrated wisdom. They can encourage and motivate you to hold fast to your convictions.

LUKE 16:10 | *If you are faithful in little things, you will be faithful in large ones. But if you are dishonest in little things, you won't be honest with greater responsibilities.*

Living by right convictions begins with small decisions and choices made when no one else is watching.

How do I make sure that I won't fall back into my old patterns?

PSALM 27:1-3 | *The LORD is my light and my salvation—so why should I be afraid? The LORD is my fortress, protecting me from danger, so why should I tremble? When evil people come to devour me, when my enemies and foes attack me, they will stumble and fall. Though a mighty army surrounds me, my heart will not be afraid. Even if I am attacked, I will remain confident.*

ROMANS 8:31-32 | *If God is for us, who can ever be against us? Since he did not spare even his own Son but gave him up for us all, won't he also give us everything else?*

If you are worried that you will stumble back into your old lifestyle, think about the reason why you decided to quit bad habits. God instilled in you the conviction to change and helped motivate you to start the process. He did this because he desires a relationship with you, and he will do anything to make this relationship with you strong. He will not let you fall back into addiction if you commit to relying on his help. Ask him to help you and depend on him to help you—he will.

Should I work with a counselor?

1 CHRONICLES 27:32 | *Jonathan, David's uncle, was a wise counselor to the king, a man of great insight, and a scribe.*

PROVERBS 11:14 | *Without wise leadership, a nation falls; there is safety in having many advisers.*

ISAIAH 1:26 | *[The Lord says,] "I will give you good judges again and wise counselors like you used to have. Then Jerusalem will again be called the Home of Justice and the Faithful City."*

LUKE 14:31 | *What king would go to war against another king without first sitting down with his counselors to discuss whether his army of 10,000 could defeat the 20,000 soldiers marching against him?*

One of the best things you can do to strengthen your recovery is to meet regularly with a counselor or psychologist. He or she can help you discover possible reasons for your struggles, help you identify and start healing from the pain of the past, help you learn ways to avoid new struggles, and help you find encouragement through discovering your strengths. In the Bible, counselors were viewed as people with advice of the utmost importance. Counselors and psychotherapists in modern times have proven to be extremely effective for those in the recovery process.

How will developing wisdom help me take a moral inventory of my life?

PSALM 19:7 | *The instructions of the LORD are perfect, reviving the soul. The decrees of the LORD are trustworthy, making wise the simple.*

ROMANS 12:2 | *Don't copy the behavior and customs of this world, but let God transform you into a new person by changing the way you think. Then you will learn to know God's will for you, which is good and pleasing and perfect.*

Wisdom transforms head knowledge into commonsense action. Wisdom from God helps you discern deceptive and distorted thoughts, giving you the ability to examine yourself through God's eyes and the necessary knowledge to continue through the twelve-step process.

How do I obtain wisdom?

JAMES 1:5 I *If you need wisdom, ask our generous God, and he will give it to you. He will not rebuke you for asking.*

God promises to give wisdom to anyone who asks. You don't need to be embarrassed to ask God for the wisdom and direction you need.

DEUTERONOMY 4:5-6 I *[Moses said,] "I now teach you these decrees and regulations just as the LORD my God commanded me. . . . Obey them completely, and you will display your wisdom and intelligence among the surrounding nations. When they hear all these decrees, they will exclaim, 'How wise and prudent are the people of this great nation!'"*

PROVERBS 1:5-6 I *Let the wise listen to these proverbs and become even wiser. Let those with understanding receive guidance by exploring the meaning in these proverbs and parables, the words of the wise and their riddles.*

PROVERBS 1:23 I *Come and listen to my counsel. I'll share my heart with you and make you wise.*

COLOSSIANS 3:16 I *Let the message about Christ, in all its richness, fill your lives. Teach and counsel each other with all the wisdom he gives.*

Obedience to God's Word—his commands, laws, and teachings—will make you wise. It is your most reliable source of wisdom and insight because it is the very counsel of God himself and therefore speaks to all situations, including the process of recovery.

PROVERBS 9:10 | *Fear of the LORD is the foundation of wisdom. Knowledge of the Holy One results in good judgment.*

Being in awe of God will make you wise as you consider his ways and how he wants you to conduct your life. It will keep you from making mistakes that would slow your recovery.

PROVERBS 20:18 | *Plans succeed through good counsel.*

Wisdom often comes to you through the counsel of thoughtful, godly people.

STEP 5

"We admitted to God, to ourselves, and to another human being the exact nature of our wrongs."

What is the importance of admitting my mistakes? Why should I confess my sins?

JEREMIAH 3:13 | *Acknowledge your guilt. Admit that you rebelled against the LORD your God. . . . Confess that you refused to listen to my voice. I, the LORD, have spoken!*

God commands you to admit your sins, not so that you'll be punished and exposed but so that you'll be forgiven and healed.

1 JOHN 1:10 | *If we claim we have not sinned, we are calling God a liar and showing that his word has no place in our hearts.*

Admitting your sin is agreeing with God about the nature of your wrongs and what you should do about them. Only when you recognize where you have strayed from God's path of life are you able to see how to get back on it. Then you are ready to deal with your wrongs and sin so that you can get going in the right direction again.

PSALM 51:1-2 | *Have mercy on me, O God, because of your unfailing love. Because of your great compassion, blot out the stain of my sins. Wash me clean from my guilt. Purify me from my sin.*

PROVERBS 28:13 | *People who conceal their sins will not prosper, but if they confess and turn from them, they will receive mercy.*

Trying to hide your sins will prevent you from getting rid of them, to have them washed clean by God. But when you admit your sins to God (called "confession"), he will mercifully forgive you and cleanse you on the inside, making you pure in his sight.

2 SAMUEL 12:13 | *David confessed to Nathan, "I have sinned against the LORD." Nathan replied, "Yes, but the LORD has forgiven you, and you won't die for this sin."*

PSALM 32:3, 5 | *When I refused to confess my sin, my body wasted away, and I groaned all day long. . . . Finally, I confessed all my sins to you and stopped trying to hide my guilt. I said to myself, "I will confess my rebellion to the LORD." And you forgave me! All my guilt is gone.*

To admit your mistakes and sins is to open the door to forgiveness and restoration of your relationship with God and with those you have wronged. How can you ask God to forgive your sins before you freely admit to him that you want his forgiveness, and how can you do that before you freely admit to him that you are a sinner?

JAMES 5:16 | *Confess your sins to each other and pray for each other so that you may be healed. The earnest prayer of a righteous person has great power and produces wonderful results.*

Admitting your sins to another person deepens the level of your fellowship and encourages you and the other person to pray for each other.

EZRA 10:1 | *While Ezra prayed and made this confession, weeping and lying face down on the ground in front of the Temple of God, a very large crowd of people from Israel—men, women, and children—gathered and wept bitterly with him.*

Admitting your own sins often leads others to confess and repent of theirs.

NEHEMIAH 9:3 | *They remained standing in place for three hours while the Book of the Law of the LORD their God was read aloud to them. Then for three more hours they confessed their sins and worshiped the LORD their God.*

Admitting your sins is an important part of having a heart that is free to worship the Lord.

What is involved in admitting my wrongs to God?

2 CHRONICLES 7:14 | *If my people who are called by my name will humble themselves and pray and seek my face and turn from* *their wicked ways, I will hear from heaven and will forgive their sins.*

PSALM 38:18 | *I confess my sins; I am deeply sorry for what I have done.*

PSALM 51:3-4, 6, 17 | *I recognize my rebellion; it haunts me day and night. Against you, and you alone, have I sinned; I have done what is evil in your sight. . . . You desire honesty from the womb, teaching me wisdom even there. . . . The sacrifice you desire is a broken spirit. You will not reject a broken and repentant heart, O God.*

Humbly admitting that you have sinned; being sorry for what you have done to hurt God, others, and yourself; and confessing your wrongs are the steps you should take in bringing your wrongs to God. These steps may seem very specific, but they are important to do so that you are ready for God to change you.

Why do I confess my sins to God and then to someone else?

1 CHRONICLES 21:8 | *David said to God, "I have sinned greatly by taking this census. Please forgive my guilt for doing this foolish thing."*

PSALM 51:4 | *Against you, and you alone, have I sinned; I have done what is evil in your sight.*

Any wrong you do saddens your Creator, who desires your obedience. Sometimes you sin only against God. Your thought life is an example of this. Often, however, your sins affect others in some way. Confess first to God, who always forgives; he will then give you the strength and grace to ask forgiveness of those you have wronged.

JAMES 5:16 | *Confess your sins to each other and pray for each other so that you may be healed.*

When what you've done has hurt someone else, it is essential to confess it to God and also to apologize to the person you've hurt. The reason it is important to confess to even just one person (maybe not even the person you have wronged) is that it brings healing in yourself. It is amazing the healing that comes forth just from explaining to someone else what you have done.

Why is it also necessary to admit my wrongs to a counselor or other trusted person?

ACTS 14:22 | *[Paul and Barnabas] strengthened the believers. They encouraged them to continue in the faith, reminding them that we must suffer many hardships to enter the Kingdom of God.*

ACTS 18:23 | *Paul went back through Galatia and Phrygia, visiting and strengthening all the believers.*

Admitting your wrongs to someone you trust gives you encouragement. When you are down, you need others to lift you up.

LUKE 17:3 | *Watch yourselves! If another believer sins, rebuke that person; then if there is repentance, forgive.*

1 CORINTHIANS 5:12 | *It isn't my responsibility to judge outsiders, but it certainly is your responsibility to judge those inside the church who are sinning.*

It provides you accountability. When you are headed in the wrong direction, you need others to help you go the right way and to help you see through your blind spots.

ACTS 12:5 | *While Peter was in prison, the church prayed very earnestly for him.*

You need their prayers. When you are in trouble, you need others to ask God to help you.

1 CORINTHIANS 12:20-22, 25 | *There are many parts, but only one body. The eye can never say to the hand, "I don't need you." The head can't say to the feet, "I don't need you." In fact, some parts of the body that seem weakest and least important are actually the most necessary. . . . This makes for harmony among the members, so that all the members care for each other.*

You receive their loving care. When life is coming apart, you need others to help you glue it back together.

STEP 6

"We were entirely ready to have God remove all these defects of character."

How can my life become more pleasing to God?

ROMANS 12:1-2 | *Give your bodies to God because of all he has done for you. Let them be a living and holy sacrifice—the kind he will find acceptable. This is truly the way to worship him. Don't copy the behavior and customs of this world, but let God transform you into a new person by changing the way you think. Then you will learn to know God's will for you, which is good and pleasing and perfect.*

Give your life to God so he can change it from the inside out. He will renew your mind, heart, and soul, giving you the spiritual insight to see what he wants you to do and how to live out your life.

What is repentance? Why does God want me to repent?

EZEKIEL 18:30-32 | *Repent, and turn from your sins. Don't let them destroy you! Put all your rebellion behind you, and find yourselves a new heart and a new spirit. For why should you die, O people of Israel? I don't want you to die, says the Sovereign LORD. Turn back and live!*

MATTHEW 3:2 | *Repent of your sins and turn to God, for the Kingdom of Heaven is near.*

ACTS 3:19 | *Repent of your sins and turn to God, so that your sins may be wiped away.*

1 CORINTHIANS 15:22 | *Just as everyone dies because we all belong to Adam, everyone who belongs to Christ will be given new life.*

2 CORINTHIANS 5:17 | *Anyone who belongs to Christ has become a new person. The old life is gone; a new life has begun!*

GALATIANS 2:20 | *My old self has been crucified with Christ. It is no longer I who live, but Christ lives in me.*

Repentance is turning *from* your wrong way of living and turning *to* God's way of living. Repentance allows you to receive a new life from God—literally, a life where the very Spirit of God lives within you. When you have made up your mind to turn from the things that you struggle with, repentance is the step you take to let God know you are ready for him to remove the defects of your character that were causing you to struggle on your own.

MATTHEW 16:24 | *Jesus said to his disciples, "If any of you wants to be my follower, you must turn from your selfish ways, take up your cross, and follow me."*

LUKE 24:47 | *There is forgiveness of sins for all who repent.*

ACTS 2:37-38 | *Peter's words pierced their hearts, and they said to him and to the other apostles, "Brothers, what should we do?" Peter replied, "Each of you must repent of your sins and turn to God, and be baptized in the name of Jesus Christ for the forgiveness of your sins. Then you will receive the gift of the Holy Spirit."*

Repentance allows you to receive forgiveness for your sins. If you are sincere when you come to God, he is always willing to forgive your sins.

Should I have a spiritual mentor?

2 KINGS 11:17 | *Jehoiada made a covenant between the LORD and the king and the people that they would be the LORD's people.*

Jehoiada's guidance made King Joash's rule successful. When Jehoiada died, instead of finding another godly adviser and confidant, Joash tried to govern on his own but failed (see 2 Chronicles 24:2, 17-18). A mentor—sometimes called a spiritual counselor or discipler—is a mature believer who will keep you accountable and supply wise guidance and encouragement. Meeting regularly and being completely honest with your mentor are essential. A mentor is not someone who punishes you when you make a mistake but rather listens to you and guides you. Mentorship is one of God's methods to develop spiritual maturity. God provided Elijah for Elisha, Barnabas for Paul, and Paul for Timothy (see 1 Kings 19:19-21; Acts 9:26-27; 16:1-3). Don't make Joash's mistake; find a mentor who can help you grow in your relationship with God.

What makes me acceptable to God?

ROMANS 3:27 | *Can we boast, then, that we have done anything to be accepted by God? No, because our acquittal is not based on obeying the law. It is based on faith.*

COLOSSIANS 2:6 | *Just as you accepted Christ Jesus as your Lord, you must continue to follow him.*

No one can earn God's acceptance because nothing you do could ever compensate for your sin. The only way to be accepted by God is to believe that his Son, Jesus, died to pay the penalty for your sins so that you could be free to enjoy eternal life with him. When you accept God's forgiveness and allow him to be Lord of your life, he completely accepts you into his presence. It's that simple.

GALATIANS 2:16 | *A person is made right with God by faith in Jesus Christ, not by obeying the law. And we have believed in Christ Jesus, so that we might be made right with God because of our faith in Christ, not because we have obeyed the law. For no one will ever be made right with God by obeying the law.*

Your sin separates you from a holy and perfect God. When you place your faith in Jesus, he removes your sin, which makes you holy and acceptable in God's sight—not because you have become perfect but because he has forgiven you.

You don't need to obey rules in order to be saved; you simply need to believe in Jesus and the fact that he will forgive you if you ask him.

Why does God want to help me?

PSALM 103:13 | *The LORD is like a father to his children, tender and compassionate to those who fear him.*

ROMANS 1:7 | *You . . . are loved by God and are called to be his own holy people. May God our Father and the Lord Jesus Christ give you grace and peace.*

1 THESSALONIANS 1:4 | *God loves you and has chosen you to be his own.*

1 JOHN 3:1 | *See how very much our Father loves us, for he calls us his children, and that is what we are!*

God is looking for a personal relationship with each person he has created. He pursues you, not to get something from you but to give wonderful gifts to you—help, hope, power, salvation, joy, peace, and eternal life. No wonder he pursues you—he knows how much these gifts can transform your life forever.

STEP 7

"We humbly asked God to remove our shortcomings."

What is true humility?

PSALM 51:3-4 | *I recognize my rebellion; it haunts me day and night. Against you, and you alone, have I sinned; I have done what is evil in your sight. You will be proved right in what you say, and your judgment against me is just.*

Humility is willingness to admit and confess sin.

PHILIPPIANS 2:5-8 | *You must have the same attitude that Christ Jesus had. Though he was God, he did not think of equality with God as something to cling to. Instead, he gave up his divine privileges; he took the humble position of a slave and was born as a human being. When he appeared in human form, he humbled himself in obedience to God and died a criminal's death on a cross.*

Humility is not thinking too highly of yourself. It is the pathway to serving God and others.

How can humility help me in times of trouble?

DANIEL 10:12 | *[The man in the vision] said, "Don't be afraid, Daniel. Since the first day you began to pray for understanding and to humble yourself before your God, your request has been heard in heaven. I have come in answer to your prayer."*

1 PETER 5:6-7 | *Humble yourselves under the mighty power of God, and at the right time he will lift you up in honor. Give all your worries and cares to God, for he cares about you.*

Pride can keep you from seeking the help you need. Humility gives you the wisdom and courage to admit your needs in any situation. You won't get help—from God or others—if you can't admit you have a problem.

How do I change the areas in my life that need to be changed?

PSALM 51:10 | *Create in me a clean heart, O God. Renew a loyal spirit within me.*

ROMANS 12:2 | *Don't copy the behavior and customs of this world, but let God transform you into a new person by changing the way you think. Then you will learn to know God's will for you, which is good and pleasing and perfect.*

EPHESIANS 4:23-24 | *Let the Spirit renew your thoughts and attitudes. Put on your new nature, created to be like God—truly righteous and holy.*

For real and dynamic change to occur, God has to give you a new way of thinking. Ask him to remove your old ways of thinking and to transform your heart into a new one that is more receptive to him. He will help you focus on what is true and good and right. Then you will begin to see the new you, a person who displays God's good, holy, and true spirit—a person who is able to resist what once tempted you.

MARK 4:20 | *The seed that fell on good soil represents those who hear and accept God's word and produce a harvest of thirty, sixty, or even a hundred times as much as had been planted!*

God's Word produces change only when you allow it to penetrate into your heart; you plant it securely; and by continually thinking about what it says and how that should impact your life, you let it grow to produce a harvest of good thoughts and actions.

Can God use my sinful, broken heart to bring him glory? If so, how might that happen?

JOEL 2:13 | *[The Lord said,] "Don't tear your clothing in your grief, but tear your hearts instead." Return to the LORD your God, for he is merciful and compassionate, slow to get angry and filled with unfailing love. He is eager to relent and not punish.*

Only through humility can your heart be broken over the sin in your life and over your past hurts and regrets. And only your broken heart can lead you to God. Humility is an essential starting place on the road to God because only with humility will you realize just how much you need him, his help, and his mercy.

PSALM 51:17 | *The sacrifice you desire is a broken spirit. You will not reject a broken and repentant heart, O God.*

2 CORINTHIANS 7:9-10 | *I am glad I sent [that letter], not because it hurt you, but because the pain caused you to repent and change your ways. It was the kind of sorrow God wants his people to have, so you were not harmed by us in any way. For the kind of sorrow God wants us to experience leads us away from sin and results in salvation. There's no regret for that kind of sorrow. But worldly sorrow, which lacks repentance, results in spiritual death.*

JAMES 4:9 | *Let there be tears for what you have done. Let there be sorrow and deep grief.*

Your broken heart leads you to realize and then confess your sin. When your heart breaks, it reveals the sin within and the need for God to clean you from the inside out. Only then can you turn from your old way of living toward a new way of living, one with freedom and purpose.

PSALM 30:11 | *You have turned my mourning into joyful dancing. You have taken away my clothes of mourning and clothed me with joy.*

PSALM 51:8-10 | *Oh, give me back my joy again; you have broken me—now let me rejoice. Don't keep looking at my sins. Remove the stain of my guilt. Create in me a clean heart, O God. Renew a loyal spirit within me.*

Your brokenness leads to healing, and healing leads to rejoicing. When God does his healing in your life, you will rejoice and others will rejoice with you.

STEP 8

"We made a list of all the persons we had harmed and became willing to make amends to them all."

How can I develop an attitude that wants to make amends to others?

2 CORINTHIANS 5:17 | *Anyone who belongs to Christ has become a new person. The old life is gone; a new life has begun!*

God gives you a fresh start when you come to him—only he can change your heart. Since God is willing to give you a fresh start, shouldn't you be willing to do the same for others?

PSALM 139:23-24 | *Search me, O God, and know my heart; test me and know my anxious thoughts. Point out anything in me that offends you, and lead me along the path of everlasting life.*

Ask God to examine your life, then respond positively to what he points out, knowing that this will help you rebuild your relationship with him and with others.

ROMANS 14:10, 13 | *Why do you condemn another believer? Why do you look down on another believer? Remember, we will all stand before the judgment seat of God. . . . So let's stop condemning each other. Decide instead to live in such a way that you will not cause another believer to stumble and fall.*

Instead of condemning others, demonstrate unconditional love toward them. Pray for them and forgive any wrong they have committed against you. Then watch how the power of forgiveness changes your attitude about them.

What happens when the love of Jesus fills my heart?

ROMANS 12:9-10 | *Don't just pretend to love others. Really love them. . . . Love each other with genuine affection, and take delight in honoring each other.*

EPHESIANS 3:19 | *May you experience the love of Christ, though it is too great to understand fully. Then you will be made complete with all the fullness of life and power that comes from God.*

1 JOHN 4:12 | *If we love each other, God lives in us, and his love is brought to full expression in us.*

When your heart is filled with the love of Jesus, there is little room for anything bad to enter. The Bible promises that his love is so great you can never fully understand it. But when you let his love in, it keeps growing inside you, pushing out any thoughts or sins that shouldn't be there. And when your love for him grows, so does your love for others.

STEP 9

"We made direct amends to such people wherever possible, except when to do so would injure them or others."

How can I restore broken relationships with others?

1 SAMUEL 12:3 | *Testify against me in the presence of the LORD and before his anointed one. Whose ox or donkey have I stolen? Have I ever cheated any of you? Have I ever oppressed you? Have I ever taken a bribe and perverted justice? Tell me and I will make right whatever I have done wrong.*

LUKE 15:18 | *I will go home to my father and say, "Father, I have sinned against both heaven and you."*

You need to confess your wrongdoings, not only to God but also to others you have wronged. *I'm sorry* are two very important words. Confession will remove the barriers between friends. It is also possible that you will need to make restitution in order to restore the relationship. Even though confessing and making restitution are difficult, your relationships are important and worth your efforts.

MATTHEW 5:23-24 | *If you are presenting a sacrifice at the altar in the Temple and you suddenly remember that someone has something against you, leave your sacrifice there at the altar. Go and be reconciled to that person. Then come and offer your sacrifice to God.*

Remember that forgiveness is both a decision and a process. Sometimes you must decide to forgive before you feel like it.

COLOSSIANS 3:13 | *Make allowance for each other's faults, and forgive anyone who offends you. Remember, the Lord forgave you, so you must forgive others.*

It is easy to accept those who forgive you, because you are drawn to those who forgave you. But it is possible that you are not the only one who has done wrong—those whom you have hurt could have also hurt you as they withdrew from you or punished you for your addictions. In addition, it is very important to forgive those who confess things to you. When you forgive others, you no longer see them as being against you.

Why is restitution with others necessary in my recovery process?

NUMBERS 5:7 | *They must confess their sin and make full restitution for what they have done, adding an additional 20 percent and returning it to the person who was wronged.*

LUKE 19:8-10 | *Zacchaeus stood before the Lord and said, "I will give half my wealth to the poor, Lord, and if I have cheated people on their taxes, I will give them back four times as much!" Jesus responded, "Salvation has come to this home today, for this man has shown himself to be a true son of Abraham. For the Son of Man came to seek and save those who are lost."*

Restitution is the act of making up for wrong you have done. It is an attempt to put value behind your asking for forgiveness, demonstrating seriousness about your desire to be forgiven. It acknowledges the wrong committed and shows concern for the one wronged. When you decide to try to restore a relationship with someone you have hurt, you are being responsible (even if he or she refuses to be friends again). It is through responsibility that you can start to recover effectively. Restitution is usually sufficient when it exceeds what you would expect if you were the wounded one.

MATTHEW 5:23-24 | *If you are presenting a sacrifice at the altar in the Temple and you suddenly remember that someone has something against you, leave your sacrifice there at the altar. Go and be reconciled to that person.*

MATTHEW 18:15 | *If another believer sins against you, go privately and point out the offense. If the other person listens and confesses it, you have won that person back.*

ACTS 14:21-22, 27-28 | *After preaching the Good News in Derbe and making many disciples, Paul and Barnabas returned . . . [and] strengthened the believers. They encouraged them to continue in the faith. . . . Upon arriving in Antioch, they called the church together and reported everything God had done through them and how he had opened the door of faith to the Gentiles, too. And they stayed there with the believers for a long time.*

Strong relationships promote encouragement and help for one another. The more you work at restoring relationships, the more help and encouragement you will receive from those who are once again your friends. Even though you might have hurt them, when they understand that you are sorry and want the relationship back, they will be more likely to help and encourage you in your recovery process.

GENESIS 2:18 | *The LORD God said, "It is not good for the man to be alone. I will make a helper who is just right for him."*

PSALM 133:1, 3 | *How wonderful and pleasant it is when brothers live together in harmony! . . . Harmony is as refreshing as the dew from Mount Hermon that falls on the mountains of Zion. And there the LORD has pronounced his blessing, even life everlasting.*

PROVERBS 17:17 | *A friend is always loyal, and a brother is born to help in time of need.*

God uses your relationships to bless you. Harmonious relationships are refreshing, restoring your soul. God made you to need others, and others to need you, so it is wise to restore the relationships you have broken.

How can I make peace with others?

PSALM 34:14-15 | *Turn away from evil and do good. Search for peace, and work to maintain it. The eyes of the LORD watch over those who do right; his ears are open to their cries for help.*

Pursuing peace with others is the right thing to do; therefore, God will bless your efforts. You can therefore pray confidently for him to change your heart and to touch the lives of those with whom you want to be reconciled.

EPHESIANS 4:3 | *Make every effort to keep yourselves united in the Spirit, binding yourselves together with peace.*

After you have confessed to others the wrongs you have done, you can unite with them in the realization that you have the same goal: working together to please God.

STEP 10

"We continued to take personal inventory, and when we were wrong, promptly admitted it."

Do I practice living the way Jesus did?

PSALM 119:34 | *Give me understanding and I will obey your instructions; I will put them into practice with all my heart.*

HEBREWS 6:1-3 | *Let us stop going over the basic teachings about Christ again and again. Let us go on instead and become mature in our understanding. Surely we don't need to start again with the fundamental importance of repenting from evil deeds and placing our faith in God. You don't need further instruction about baptisms, the laying on of hands, the resurrection of the dead, and eternal judgment. And so, God willing, we will move forward to further understanding.*

Practice brings progress, in action and in understanding. If you are learning to play the piano, you need to learn the basics and practice them over and over. Eventually you master simple pieces, and only then are you prepared to learn pieces of greater difficulty. Each piece builds upon the previous piece, making the basics second nature while expanding your understanding of music. Practicing spiritual living is just as important for mastering the basics of following Jesus and deepening your understanding of him and his call on your life. The more you practice the disciplines of spiritual living—such as praying, studying the Bible, and serving others in need—the more you will live like Jesus did and become the kind of person God created you to be.

GENESIS 39:6-7, 10-12 | *Joseph was a very handsome and well-built young man, and Potiphar's wife soon began to look at him lustfully. "Come and sleep with me," she demanded. . . . She kept putting pressure on Joseph day after day, but he refused to sleep with her, and he kept out of her way as much as possible. One day . . . she came and grabbed him by his cloak, demanding, "Come on, sleep with me!" Joseph tore himself away, but he left his cloak in her hand as he ran from the house.*

When practicing spiritual living, you must also practice avoiding unhealthy living. Like Joseph, when practicing purity or integrity you must also practice avoiding temptation. Practicing these two concepts in tandem is important preparation for the moment temptation strikes the hardest. Then, like Joseph, you will be able to do the right thing.

What are some common mistakes I might make when taking a personal inventory of my life?

JOB 10:18-19 | *Why, then, did you deliver me from my mother's womb? Why didn't you let me die at birth? It would be as though I had never existed, going directly from the womb to the grave.*

You might sometimes doubt that God is working in your life. When you doubt God's work, you begin to doubt God, and then you begin to lose faith that he really can help you.

GENESIS 3:11-13 | *The LORD God asked . . . "Have you eaten from the tree whose fruit I commanded you not to eat?" The man replied, "It was the woman you gave me who gave me the fruit, and I ate it." Then the LORD God asked the woman, "What have you done?" "The serpent deceived me," she replied. "That's why I ate it."*

GENESIS 16:5 | *Sarai said to Abram, "This is all your fault! I put my servant into your arms, but now that she's pregnant she treats me with contempt. The LORD will show who's wrong— you or me!"*

In your pain, you might be tempted to blame others for your problems, even if the problems were self-inflicted. No matter who caused them, blaming will not bring resolution and will only delay getting to the real issue.

How can I improve my thought life?

JOSHUA 1:8 | *Study this Book of Instruction continually. Meditate on it day and night so you will be sure to obey everything written in it. Only then will you prosper and succeed in all you do.*

PROVERBS 15:14, 26, 28 | *A wise person is hungry for knowledge, while the fool feeds on trash. . . . The LORD . . . delights in pure words. . . . The heart of the godly thinks carefully before speaking.*

MARK 7:20-23 | *[Jesus said,] "It is what comes from inside that defiles you. For from within, out of a person's heart, come evil thoughts, sexual immorality, theft, murder, adultery, greed, wickedness, deceit, lustful desires, envy, slander, pride, and foolishness. All these vile things come from within; they are what defile you."*

EPHESIANS 4:17-19, 23-24 | *Live no longer as the Gentiles do, for they are hopelessly confused. Their minds are full of darkness; they wander far from the life God gives because they have closed their minds and hardened their hearts against him. They have no sense of shame. They live for lustful pleasure and eagerly practice every kind of impurity. . . . Instead, let the Spirit renew your thoughts and attitudes. Put on your new nature, created to be like God—truly righteous and holy.*

The first step to improving your thought life is to realize that what you do almost always comes from what you think about. Your conduct is shaped by your character, and your character is shaped by the condition of your heart. So if recovery is your goal, then you must change the bad thoughts your mind feeds you into new thoughts that are pure and good. When bad thoughts are trying to squeeze their way into your mind, read your Bible and recite short verses to God as prayers to help you free your mind (for example, "The Lord is my Shepherd, I will follow him. . . . The Lord is my Shepherd, I will follow him"). Improving your thought life is very important in the recovery process. Further, improving your thought life is just like recovering from an addiction: It takes time, but each day gets easier.

PSALM 19:14 | *May the words of my mouth and the meditation of my heart be pleasing to you, O LORD, my rock and my redeemer.*

PSALM 26:2 | *Put me on trial, LORD, and cross-examine me. Test my motives and my heart.*

PSALM 139:23 | *Search me, O God, and know my heart; test me and know my anxious thoughts.*

Invite God into your thought life so he can hold you more accountable. You do this the same way the psalmist did— you invite him into your mind and ask him to help you resist bad thoughts each time they appear.

How can I make good decisions?

PSALM 119:24 | *Your laws please me; they give me wise advice.*

PSALM 119:105 | *Your word is a lamp to guide my feet and a light for my path.*

ROMANS 2:18 | *You know what [God] wants; you know what is right because you have been taught his law.*

2 TIMOTHY 3:16 | *All Scripture is inspired by God and is useful to teach us what is true and to make us realize what is wrong in our lives. It corrects us when we are wrong and teaches us to do what is right.*

Start by making the basic and obvious decisions to do what the Bible says is right and to avoid what the Bible says is wrong. Knowing the Bible and gleaning its wisdom give you more options in your decision making and provide you with the discernment you need to make healthy choices. A right decision is one that is consistent with the principles of truth found in God's Word. If only one of your possible choices would please God, that is the right decision. If there are several choices, all of which are consistent with

God's Word, the most important thing may be the process of trusting God to help you make the most of the path you choose.

PSALM 25:4 | *Show me the right path, O LORD; point out the road for me to follow.*

PROVERBS 3:5-6 | *Trust in the LORD with all your heart; do not depend on your own understanding. Seek his will in all you do, and he will show you which path to take.*

Talking with God calms your spirit and clears your mind, thereby helping you make good decisions. Learn how to trust him and how to be open with him, and he will guide you through every decision.

PSALM 37:30 | *The godly offer good counsel; they teach right from wrong.*

PROVERBS 12:15 | *Fools think their own way is right, but the wise listen to others.*

Much of your decision making is based on the advice you glean from others. Start listening to advice from people who have experience helping others through recovery and who faithfully and consistently follow God. Then carefully consider this advice as you make your decisions.

MATTHEW 16:26 | *What do you benefit if you gain the whole world but lose your own soul? Is anything worth more than your soul?*

Resist the temptation to make choices guided only by a desire for personal satisfaction. Although one bad decision might not lead you down the wrong road, it can be the first of many more bad decisions. Remember your past before you make a decision.

How can I exercise self-control over my negative emotions?

PROVERBS 4:23 | *Guard your heart above all else, for it determines the course of your life.*

EZEKIEL 36:26 | *I will give you a new heart, and I will put a new spirit in you. I will take out your stony, stubborn heart and give you a tender, responsive heart.*

Your emotions, which are God-given and are not bad in and of themselves, are constantly influenced by your sinful nature. This should make you cautious about trusting your emotions, because Satan is trying to get you to think that your sinful feelings are right. It is obvious, then, that guarding your heart means not allowing bad influences in. For example, by looking at pornography, you let it into your mind and heart; the healthy emotion of love becomes tainted, turns to lust, and convinces you that you deserve to enjoy that sinful pleasure. To effectively exercise self-control over your emotions, you must be able to discern between right and wrong emotions. By reading and knowing the Bible, your mind and heart become attuned to what God thinks is right, which helps your recovery.

PROVERBS 16:32 | *Better to be patient than powerful; better to have self-control than to conquer a city.*

PROVERBS 25:28 | *A person without self-control is like a city with broken-down walls.*

1 PETER 1:13-16 I *Think clearly and exercise self-control. Look forward to the gracious salvation that will come to you when Jesus Christ is revealed to the world. So you must live as God's obedient children. Don't slip back into your old ways of living to satisfy your own desires. You didn't know any better then. But now you must be holy in everything you do, just as God who chose you is holy. For the Scriptures say, "You must be holy because I am holy."*

Try to recognize the specific negative emotions that tend to control you. This is the first step in not letting them take hold of you. It is at the beginning of negative emotions that you can best stand up against them and exercise control over them, rather than letting them take control of you.

JOB 7:11 I *I cannot keep from speaking. I must express my anguish.*

Keep an open dialogue with the Lord and others you trust so that you are not covering up your emotions. If you ask, God will remind you when you feel the beginning of negative emotions and will show you a way out of dwelling on them. And your friends can hold you accountable by periodically asking you about your negative emotions.

If God created everyone with a conscience, why do I have such a hard time listening to mine?

1 TIMOTHY 1:19 I *Cling to your faith in Christ, and keep your conscience clear. For some people have deliberately violated their consciences; as a result, their faith has been shipwrecked.*

Sin is an act of going against your conscience. You know that what you are doing is wrong because your conscience tells you so, but you do it anyway because it is so appealing. If you consistently go against what your conscience tells you, you can train yourself to not hear it warning you of danger. In a sense you have "tricked" your conscience into thinking all is well when it really isn't. Eventually, you become insensitive to sin. Listening to your conscience is a good way to keep away from sin. And doing your best to keep away from sin is the best way to keep a clear conscience.

I have dulled my conscience. Can it be restored?

HOSEA 12:6 I *Come back to your God. Act with love and justice, and always depend on him.*

When you recommit yourself to God and again live by the commands in his Word, the Bible, he will restore your conscience. It will be strong enough to help you avoid temptation and will help you do the things needed for recovery.

STEP 11

"We sought through prayer and quietness to improve our contact with God, praying only for knowledge of his will for us and the power to carry that out."

Why is prayer important?

MATTHEW 7:7-11 I *Keep on asking, and you will receive what you ask for. Keep on seeking, and you will find. Keep on knocking, and the door will be opened to you. For everyone who asks, receives. Everyone who seeks, finds. And to everyone who knocks, the door will be opened. You parents—if your children ask for a loaf of bread, do you give them a stone instead? Or if they ask for a fish, do you give them a snake? Of course not! So if you sinful people know how to give good gifts to your children, how much more will your heavenly Father give good gifts to those who ask him.*

There's more to prayer than just getting an answer to a question or a solution for a problem. God often does more in your heart through the act of praying than he does in actually answering your prayers. As you persist in talking and listening to God, you will gain a greater understanding of yourself, your situation, your motivation to recover, and God's nature and direction for your life.

Does God always answer prayer?

PSALM 116:1-2 | *I love the LORD because he hears my voice and my prayer for mercy. Because he bends down to listen, I will pray as long as I have breath!*

1 PETER 3:12 | *The eyes of the Lord watch over those who do right, and his ears are open to their prayers. But the Lord turns his face against those who do evil.*

Yes, God listens carefully to every prayer and answers it. His answer may be yes, no, or wait. A yes answer to every request would spoil you. A no answer to every request would be discouraging to your spirit. Making you wait for the answer to every prayer would be frustrating. God always answers based on what he knows is best for you. When you don't get the answer you want, your spiritual maturity will grow as you learn to trust that God's answer is in your best interest.

Does God really have a specific plan for my life? Can I mess it up?

PSALM 138:8 | *The LORD will work out his plans for my life.*

JEREMIAH 1:5 | *I knew you before I formed you in your mother's womb. Before you were born I set you apart and appointed you.*

ROMANS 8:28 | *God causes everything to work together for the good of those who love God and are called according to his purpose for them.*

If God does have a plan for your life, how do you know what it is and whether you are following it? The first step is simply to accept that God does have a plan for you. Without this first step of faith, you will miss everything God does to get your attention. Next, open your eyes—your spiritual eyes. Notice the people who come into your life, who cross your path during the day. These are potentially people God wants to use in your life or wants you to minister to. Act on what and whom God places in front of you, and you will follow his plan for your life, day by day, month by month, year by year. Your life will always have a sense of mystery because you can't know the future, but if you act upon each situation God puts in front of you, your life will not seem random nor will it seem like an automated script you must follow. When you are always watching for God's work in your life, you will train yourself to notice it and recognize it for what it is.

How can I know what God is telling me to do with my life?

ROMANS 12:6 | *In his grace, God has given us different gifts for doing certain things well.*

1 CORINTHIANS 12:7 | *A spiritual gift is given to each of us so we can help each other.*

1 CORINTHIANS 12:11 | *It is the one and only Spirit who distributes all these gifts. He alone decides which gift each person should have.*

What passions do you have? What things are you good at and what do you like to do? God planted these things in your heart so that you might use them for his purpose. People do things better when the task is related to a passion, and people feel more fulfilled in life when they are using their passionate skills for good. God knows this, and he designed humans to feel extreme joy and purpose about their passions. So discover what you really like to do, see that as God's gift to you, and use those passions to serve him and do good for others.

Will God use me in spite of my inadequacies and failures?

EXODUS 2:12 | *After looking in all directions to make sure no one was watching, Moses killed the Egyptian and hid the body in the sand.*

JUDGES 16:17, 21, 28 | *Finally, Samson shared his secret with her. . . . So the Philistines captured him and gouged out his eyes. . . . Then Samson prayed to the LORD, "Sovereign LORD, remember me again."*

JONAH 1:3 | *Jonah . . . went in the opposite direction to get away from the LORD.*

MATTHEW 26:69-70 | *Peter was sitting outside in the courtyard. A servant girl came over and said to him, "You were one of those with Jesus the Galilean." But Peter denied it in front of everyone. "I don't know what you're talking about," he said.*

Fortunately, God does holy work through unholy people—he knows no one is perfect. Perfection is not a requirement for you to be used by God. He can use anyone he chooses and any circumstance to bring about his will. In the verses above, you read about the great failures of Moses, Samson, Jonah, and Peter. Yet God used each of them in a mighty way to carry out his work and his plans. God knew the future sins of these men when he set them apart to become his leaders. But he also knew that these men longed to have a clean heart and a right relationship with God, even though they often stumbled in their faith. The key to your being used by God is not perfection but a willingness to be forgiven, to turn from sin, and to serve God with humility as best as you can.

STEP 12

"Having had a spiritual awakening as the result of these steps, we tried to carry this message to others and to practice these principles in all we do."

How do I develop more consistency in my walk with God?

JOHN 14:15 | *[Jesus said,] "If you love me, obey my commandments."*

JOHN 15:10-11 I *[Jesus said,] "When you obey my command-ments, you remain in my love. . . . I have told you these things so that you will be filled with my joy. Yes, your joy will overflow!"*

Practice obeying. Think daily about following the commands in God's Word. When you regularly obey his instructions for living, you will avoid many of the things that can hurt you and you will find joy in a closer relation-ship with him.

MICAH 6:8 I *O people, the LORD has told you what is good, and this is what he requires of you: to do what is right, to love mercy, and to walk humbly with your God.*

Develop a desire to obey God. If you have children, you know they usually try to obey because they *want* to please you, even if they don't always achieve it. That is what God is looking for. He knows that because of your sinful nature, you won't always obey him. What he wants is your *desire* to obey, because that is the sign that you love and respect him, that you believe his way for you is best. If you consistently disobey because you enjoy it, you do not yet love God the way he wants you to.

How do I carry my message of spiritual awakening to others? What does it include?

EXODUS 18:8 I *Moses told his father-in-law everything the LORD had done to Pharaoh and Egypt on behalf of Israel. He also told about all the hardships they had experienced along the way and how the LORD had rescued his people from all their troubles.*

JOHN 9:25 | *The man [said,] "I know this: I was blind, and now I can see!"*

ROMANS 1:16 | *I am not ashamed of this Good News about Christ. It is the power of God at work, saving everyone who believes.*

ROMANS 7:24-25 | *Oh, what a miserable person I am! Who will free me from this life that is dominated by sin and death? Thank God! The answer is in Jesus Christ our Lord. So you see how it is: In my mind I really want to obey God's law, but because of my sinful nature I am a slave to sin.*

COLOSSIANS 1:13-14 | *[God] has rescued us from the kingdom of darkness and transferred us into the Kingdom of his dear Son, who purchased our freedom and forgave our sins.*

2 TIMOTHY 1:1 | *I have been sent out to tell others about the life [God] has promised through faith in Christ Jesus.*

It includes telling others how God has rescued you and freed you from the burden of addiction.

PSALM 28:6 | *Praise the LORD! For he has heard my cry for mercy.*

PSALM 138:3 | *As soon as I pray, you answer me; you encourage me by giving me strength.*

It includes telling others about the prayers God has answered.

PSALM 30:3 | *You brought me up from the grave, O LORD. You kept me from falling into the pit of death.*

JOHN 3:16 | *God loved the world so much that he gave his one and only Son, so that everyone who believes in him will not perish but have eternal life.*

It includes explaining how God has saved you from spiritual death.

ROMANS 6:23 | *The wages of sin is death, but the free gift of God is eternal life through Christ Jesus our Lord.*

It includes telling others the terrific news that anyone can have the gift of eternal life. It's not too good to be true!

ACTS 4:33 | *The apostles testified powerfully to the resurrection of the Lord Jesus, and God's great blessing was upon them all.*

It includes telling others about the resurrection of Jesus, for this is the basis for a believer's hope in eternal life.

LUKE 24:47 | *There is forgiveness of sins for all who repent.*

ROMANS 5:1 | *Since we have been made right in God's sight by faith, we have peace with God because of what Jesus Christ our Lord has done for us.*

It includes explaining the message of repentance, forgiveness, and reconciliation with God.

2 TIMOTHY 4:5 | *Work at telling others the Good News, and fully carry out the ministry God has given you.*

It includes persistence and endurance as you stay focused on living for Jesus and following him wherever he leads you.

1 THESSALONIANS 1:5 | *When we brought you the Good News, it was not only with words but also with power, for the Holy Spirit gave you full assurance that what we said was true. And you know of our concern for you from the way we lived when we were with you.*

It includes relying on God's Holy Spirit to help you make your actions match your words.

How can I can stay close to God and prevent spiritual dryness?

PSALM 63:1 | *O God, you are my God; I earnestly search for you. My soul thirsts for you; my whole body longs for you in this parched and weary land where there is no water.*

PSALM 143:6 | *I lift my hands to you in prayer. I thirst for you as parched land thirsts for rain.*

JOHN 6:35 | *Jesus [said], "I am the bread of life. Whoever comes to me will never be hungry again. Whoever believes in me will never be thirsty."*

REVELATION 22:17 | *The Spirit and the bride say, "Come." Let anyone who hears this say, "Come." Let anyone who is thirsty come. Let anyone who desires drink freely from the water of life.*

Trees by a riverbank grow full and tall. In the same way, if you stay close to God you will grow to spiritual maturity. You will not hunger or thirst for meaning in life, because God will nourish you with his Word and his presence.

PROVERBS 4:23 | *Guard your heart above all else, for it determines the course of your life.*

1 JOHN 5:21 | *Keep away from anything that might take God's place in your hearts.*

Keep sin from controlling your life. It is when you let God have control of your life that you become spiritually mature, and the things of the past will not tempt you the way they once did.

PSALM 32:3-4 | *When I refused to confess my sin, my body wasted away, and I groaned all day long. Day and night your hand of discipline was heavy on me. My strength evaporated like water in the summer heat.*

1 JOHN 1:9 | *If we confess our sins to him, he is faithful and just to forgive us our sins and to cleanse us.*

Confess any sin right away, asking God to forgive you and turn your heart back toward him. Each time you do this, your soul will be cleansed and you will feel renewed.

PHILIPPIANS 2:4 | *Don't look out only for your own interests, but take an interest in others, too.*

HEBREWS 6:11-12 | *Our great desire is that you will keep on loving others as long as life lasts, in order to make certain that what you hope for will come true. Then you will not become spiritually dull and indifferent.*

Practice genuine, active love for the people around you. Try to understand them—it is amazing how you learn to love people when you realize they are all going through problems, distractions, losses, and hardships just like you are. This nonjudgmental love for others will refresh your soul as well as those you love.

ISAIAH 58:11 | *The LORD will guide you continually, giving you water when you are dry and restoring your strength. You will be like a well-watered garden, like an ever-flowing spring.*

HEBREWS 2:1 | *We must listen very carefully to the truth we have heard, or we may drift away from it.*

Live in obedience to God's truth. Reading the Bible will help you know that truth and will affect you positively, even if you don't always feel like reading it.

DEUTERONOMY 6:11-12 | *When you have eaten your fill in this land, be careful not to forget the LORD, who rescued you.*

HOSEA 13:5-6 | *I took care of you in the wilderness, in that dry and thirsty land. But when you had eaten and were satisfied, you became proud and forgot me.*

When you are in need, you are likely to turn to God. But when you are well fed, comfortable, and prosperous, it is easy to become complacent about him. Make sure that you remember him after you've recovered. And make sure that you come out on the other end with an even closer relationship to God. That way, your faith will be so strong that you will not think about going back into your addiction, for your life will have too much purpose to go back.

ROMANS 12:11 | *Never be lazy, but work hard and serve the Lord enthusiastically.*

COLOSSIANS 3:23 | *Work willingly at whatever you do, as though you were working for the Lord rather than for people.*

2 JOHN 1:8 | *Watch out that you do not lose what we have worked so hard to achieve. Be diligent so that you receive your full reward.*

Work diligently and enthusiastically for the Lord. Serving God refreshes your soul and gives you purpose.

What happens if spiritual dryness continues in my life?

PHILIPPIANS 1:6 | *God, who began the good work within you, will continue his work until it is finally finished on the day when Christ Jesus returns.*

COLOSSIANS 3:10 | *Put on your new nature, and be renewed as you learn to know your Creator and become like him.*

A great work takes a long time to complete. Though you were converted in a moment of faith, the process of transformation into Christlikeness takes a lifetime. While it may appear slow to you, God's work is unrelenting and certain.

How can I find contentment, regardless of life's circumstances?

2 CORINTHIANS 12:10 | *I take pleasure in my weaknesses, and in the insults, hardships, persecutions, and troubles that I suffer for Christ. For when I am weak, then I am strong.*

PHILIPPIANS 4:11-13 | *I have learned how to be content with whatever I have. I know how to live on almost nothing or with everything. I have learned the secret of living in every situation, whether it is with a full stomach or empty, with plenty or little. For I can do everything through Christ, who gives me strength.*

2 PETER 1:3 | *By his divine power, God has given us everything we need for living a godly life. We have received all of this by coming to know him, the one who called us to himself by means of his marvelous glory and excellence.*

Many think true contentment takes place only when everything in life is going well. But when contentment depends on things going your way, you are unhappy when things don't. If, instead, your contentment comes from letting Jesus meet your needs, you are secure and happy because he never fails you. The things you *want* in life may not be the best for you, so Jesus teaches you to discern the valuable things in life from the distractions—to separate your needs from your wants. This is not always the easiest lesson to learn, but the feeling of contentment you get when you let Christ provide for you is like no other.

PSALM 90:14 | *Satisfy us each morning with your unfailing love, so we may sing for joy to the end of our lives.*

PSALM 107:8-9 | *Let them praise the LORD for his great love and for the wonderful things he has done for them. For he satisfies the thirsty and fills the hungry with good things.*

Contentment comes from the assurance that God loves you unconditionally. Nothing you do can make him love you less, and no matter how hard you try, he couldn't love you more.

How can I regain my enthusiasm for life?

PSALM 19:1 | *The heavens proclaim the glory of God. The skies display his craftsmanship.*

An iridescent sunset, the tiny veins of a leaf, or a fresh breeze can lift your spirits if you take a moment to let yourself wonder at God's creation. Once you have been off your substance of choice for a while, your senses will start to surprise you, letting you smell, taste, see, hear, and touch things with renewed appreciation.

PSALM 103:2 | *Let all that I am praise the LORD; may I never forget the good things he does for me.*

No matter how bad your life has been, God has still given you much to be thankful for. If you forget about these things, you will have no passion for life. If you remember to thank God often for what you have, your passion for life will grow.

PROVERBS 12:25 | *Worry weighs a person down; an encouraging word cheers a person up.*

2 CORINTHIANS 9:2 | *It was your enthusiasm that stirred up many of the . . . believers to begin giving.*

Have you ever noticed that when you're around a friend who smiles a lot, you start to smile more too? Choose to spend more time with people like this. Not only will their smiles rub off on you, but their enthusiasm will, as well.

PSALM 9:2 | *I will be filled with joy because of you. I will sing praises to your name, O Most High.*

It is hard to do things you don't want to do. But if you tell God how amazing he is—even when you don't feel like it—your joy will miraculously increase and you will have motivation to do what you didn't want to do.

MATTHEW 4:19 | *Jesus called out . . ., "Come, follow me, and I will show you how to fish for people!"*

ROMANS 11:29 | *God's gifts and his call can never be withdrawn.*

One of the greatest ways to increase your enthusiasm for life is to find the purpose God has for your life. God gave you specific abilities you're good at, and when you discover how to use them for good, your joy will greatly increase.

Part Four

Beyond the Twelve Steps—

Other Recovery Steps and Questions

ANOTHER'S ADDICTION

What should I do if I suspect addiction in another's life?

GALATIANS 6:1 | *Brothers and sisters, if another believer is over-come by some sin, you who are godly should gently and humbly help that person back onto the right path. And be careful not to fall into the same temptation yourself.*

You are to confront others with gentleness and humility. Gentleness means being compassionate while still speaking the truth in love. Humility could involve recognizing your own limitations and the need to get your friend additional, professional help.

LUKE 10:34-35 | *The Samaritan soothed [the man's] wounds with olive oil and wine and bandaged them. Then he put the man on his own donkey and took him to an inn, where he took care of him. The next day he handed the innkeeper two silver coins, telling him, "Take care of this man. If his bill runs higher than this, I'll pay you the next time I'm here."*

ROMANS 12:13 | *When God's people are in need, be ready to help them.*

You are to help others by way of a relationship, not by avoidance. Your relationship with those caught in addiction might be what leads them out of trouble and back to God, who is the only One who can free people from the addiction of sin. Hopefully your own story of overcoming a struggle can be an example of how God's grace and love will help them, as well.

FORGIVENESS

How can I ever forgive someone who has hurt me deeply?

MATTHEW 5:44 | *Love your enemies! Pray for those who persecute you!*

COLOSSIANS 3:13 | *Make allowance for each other's faults, and forgive anyone who offends you. Remember, the Lord forgave you, so you must forgive others.*

1 PETER 3:8-9 | *All of you should be of one mind. Sympathize with each other. Love each other as brothers and sisters. Be tenderhearted, and keep a humble attitude. Don't repay evil for evil. Don't retaliate with insults when people insult you. Instead, pay them back with a blessing. That is what God has called you to do, and he will bless you for it.*

If you are looking to recover, forgiving everyone who has hurt you or caused you to stumble is necessary. This may be one of the hardest things you do because you may still be living with the consequences of the hurt. However, forgiveness is necessary in order to recover because it lets go of the bitterness and hatred. They would make recovery virtually impossible, while forgiveness will restore and revive your heart.

MATTHEW 18:21-22 | *Peter . . . asked, "Lord, how often should I forgive someone who sins against me? Seven times?" "No, not seven times," Jesus replied, "but seventy times seven!"*

Just as God forgives you without limit, you should forgive others without counting the number of times you have to forgive them. Think of how much God loves you. Now think of how many times you sin against him. Although your sins against God—who loves you so much— are without number, he still forgives you. Every time. Remember this when you are debating whether to forgive people for what they have done to you.

LUKE 23:34 | *Jesus said, "Father, forgive them, for they don't know what they are doing."*

Jesus forgave those who mocked him and killed him. He was more concerned about his offenders' relationship with God than about his own pain. Many of the people who've hurt you aren't aware they have done anything wrong to you (which suggests that you have probably hurt people without knowing it, as well). Follow Jesus' example by forgiving them whether they realize what they have done or not.

ROMANS 12:19 | *Never take revenge. Leave that to the righteous anger of God. For the Scriptures say, "I will take revenge; I will pay them back," says the LORD.*

If you are wondering whether someone who has hurt you will be punished for it, you are wondering amiss. That kind of thought will eat away at you and destroy you. Let God be the judge. He will decide the consequences for every sin. Accept this and remove yourself from your bitterness and anger by forgiving the person. Then you no longer have to sit in judgment—you can enjoy the freedom that comes from a forgiving heart.

HEALTH

How will improving my health help in recovery?

1 CORINTHIANS 3:16-17 | *Don't you realize that all of you together are the temple of God and that the Spirit of God lives in you? God will destroy anyone who destroys this temple. For God's temple is holy, and you are that temple.*

Your body was created and designed by God. Taking his advice about keeping your body healthy and pure is a good idea because he knows most about it and it is his home. When you start taking the steps needed to improve your body and your health, you will find your journey toward recovery easier—when the body starts to improve, so does the mind.

How can I improve my health?

PROVERBS 14:30 | *A peaceful heart leads to a healthy body.*

ISAIAH 40:30-31 | *Even youths will become weak and tired, and young men will fall in exhaustion. But those who trust in the LORD will find new strength. They will soar high on wings like eagles. They will run and not grow weary. They will walk and not faint.*

MATTHEW 6:25-27 | *[Do not] worry about everyday life—whether you have enough food and drink, or enough clothes to wear. Isn't life more than food, and your body more than clothing? Look at the birds. They don't plant or harvest or store food in barns, for your heavenly Father feeds them. And aren't you far more valuable to him than they are?*

LUKE 12:25-27 | *Can all your worries add a single moment to your life? And if worry can't accomplish a little thing like that, what's the use of worrying over bigger things? Look at the lilies and how they grow. They don't work or make their clothing, yet Solomon in all his glory was not dressed as beautifully as they are.*

PHILIPPIANS 3:13 | *I focus on this one thing: Forgetting the past and looking forward to what lies ahead.*

Worrying about the past, present, and future takes away your energy because worry and stress actually produce negative physical effects on the immune system in the body. You can't change the things that are out of your control, so stop worrying and turn your worries into trusting that God will help you, care for you, and comfort you no matter what happens. God really does know what is best for you, and realizing that will help you stop worrying and give you energy to focus on recovery.

GENESIS 2:1-3 | *The creation of the heavens and the earth and everything in them was completed. On the seventh day God had finished his work of creation, so he rested from all his work. And God blessed the seventh day and declared it holy, because it was the day when he rested from all his work of creation.*

EXODUS 20:8-10 | *Remember to observe the Sabbath day by keeping it holy. You have six days each week for your ordinary work, but the seventh day is a Sabbath day of rest dedicated to the LORD your God.*

EXODUS 23:12 | *You have six days each week for your ordinary work, but on the seventh day you must stop working. This gives your ox and your donkey a chance to rest. It also allows your slaves and the foreigners living among you to be refreshed.*

EXODUS 31:17 | *In six days the LORD made heaven and earth, but on the seventh day he stopped working and was refreshed.*

God encourages times of rest. Rest renews you not only mentally and physically but emotionally as well, giving you more energy for the work ahead. Rest is not only a necessity but a gift from God you can accept and enjoy. Regular rest is an important part of avoiding and recovering from burnout.

TEMPTATION

Is temptation sin?

MATTHEW 4:1 | *Jesus was led by the Spirit into the wilderness to be tempted there by the devil.*

HEBREWS 4:15 | *This High Priest of ours [Jesus] understands our weaknesses, for he faced all of the same testings we do, yet he did not sin.*

Jesus was severely tempted, yet he never gave in to temptation. Since Jesus was tempted and remained sinless, we know that being tempted is not the same as sinning. You don't have to feel guilty about the temptations you wrestle with. Rather, you can devote yourself to resisting them.

MEMORIES

What do I do with bad memories?

GENESIS 41:51 | *Joseph . . . said, "God has made me forget all my troubles."*

ISAIAH 54:4 | *Fear not; you will no longer live in shame. Don't be afraid; there is no more disgrace for you. You will no longer remember the shame of your youth.*

PHILIPPIANS 3:13 | *I focus on this one thing: Forgetting the past and looking forward to what lies ahead.*

What you have gone through has probably given you bad, even haunting memories. Do these memories consume your mind? Don't worry, for just as God can help you recover from your addiction, he can help you let go of these memories. He wants you to be joyful about his unconditional love for you, so he will help you get rid of the memories that get in the way of your joy. Ask God to help clear your mind, to help you let go of these memories, and to help you focus on the present and the future with the excitement and anticipation of what he has planned for you.

CHRISTIAN COMMUNITY

Why is it important to meet together with other believers?

ACTS 4:32, 34-35 I *All the believers were united in heart and mind. And they felt that what they owned was not their own, so they shared everything they had. . . . There were no needy people among them, because those who owned land or houses would sell them and bring the money to the apostles to give to those in need.*

1 CORINTHIANS 12:4, 6-7, 11, 18, 22, 27 I *There are different kinds of spiritual gifts. . . . God works in different ways. . . . A spiritual gift is given to each of us so we can help each other. . . . It is the one and only Spirit who distributes all these gifts. He alone decides which gift each person should have. . . . Our bodies have many parts, and God has put each part just where he wants it. . . . In fact, some parts of the body that seem weakest and least important are actually the most necessary. . . . All of you together are Christ's body, and each of you is a part of it.*

EPHESIANS 4:15-16 I *We will speak the truth in love, growing in every way more and more like Christ, who is the head of his body, the church. He makes the whole body fit together perfectly. As each part does its own special work, it helps the other parts grow, so that the whole body is healthy and growing and full of love.*

Christians gather to demonstrate that, in God's church, all people from all races and classes are welcome. God's people are not distinguished by the color of their skin or the status of their jobs, but by their faith in Jesus. This unity of believers brings a wealth of collective wisdom and spiritual gifts that could never be achieved by just a few individuals.

PSALM 116:14 | *I will keep my promises to the LORD in the presence of all his people.*

MARK 6:7 | *[Jesus] called his twelve disciples together and began sending them out two by two.*

GALATIANS 6:1-2 | *Dear brothers and sisters, if another believer is overcome by some sin, you who are godly should gently and humbly help that person back onto the right path. And be careful not to fall into the same temptation yourself. Share each other's burdens, and in this way obey the law of Christ.*

Jesus created accountability by sending his disciples out in pairs. This is a wise practice to imitate, for keeping promises is easier with the accountability help of a friend. Encourage and establish relationships with others who will challenge you to maintain your standards and agree to keep a check on your conduct.

PSALM 55:14 | *What good fellowship we once enjoyed as we walked together to the house of God.*

MATTHEW 18:20 | *[Jesus said,] "Where two or three gather together as my followers, I am there among them."*

1 CORINTHIANS 5:4 | *You must call a meeting of the church. I will be present with you in spirit, and so will the power of our Lord Jesus.*

Because Jesus promises to be with his people when they gather as a body of believers, you can experience God's presence in a unique and powerful way when you meet together with other Christians.

GOALS

Are goals important?

PSALM 40:8 | *I take joy in doing your will, my God, for your instructions are written on my heart.*

Goals are fulfilling.

GALATIANS 6:9 | *Let's not get tired of doing what is good. At just the right time we will reap a harvest of blessing if we don't give up.*

PHILIPPIANS 4:13 | *I can do everything through Christ, who gives me strength.*

Goals are energizing and bring hope. They give you strength and endurance.

PROVERBS 4:25-27 | *Look straight ahead, and fix your eyes on what lies before you. Mark out a straight path for your feet; stay on the safe path. Don't get sidetracked; keep your feet from following evil.*

Goals help keep your eyes on what you are pursuing and away from temptation.

JOHN 17:1, 4 | *Jesus looked up to heaven and said, ". . . I brought glory to you here on earth by completing the work you gave me to do."*

Goals can keep you from doing too much. God is glorified not by your doing everything you can possibly do but rather by your fulfilling the goals he has for you.

WORK

Why is work important?

GENESIS 2:15 | *The LORD God placed the man in the Garden of Eden to tend and watch over it.*

EXODUS 35:35 | *The LORD has given them special skills as engravers, designers, embroiderers in blue, purple, and scarlet thread on fine linen cloth, and weavers. They excel as craftsmen and as designers.*

ROMANS 12:6 | *In his grace, God has given us different gifts for doing certain things well.*

1 CORINTHIANS 12:11 | *It is the one and only Spirit who distributes all these gifts. He alone decides which gift each person should have.*

Scripture shows that Adam and Eve worked in the Garden of Eden even before sin came into the world. This provides clues that there will be work in heaven as well. Will it be unpleasant? No, because God designed you with specific skills that you will enjoy using in heaven; but you should also be using these skills on earth! God knew which skills would make each person happy and fulfilled and would provide a purpose for life.

Part Five

Things to Avoid in Order to Recover

How do I avoid the things I'm supposed to avoid— the habits and temptations that will hurt the progress of my recovery?

PROVERBS 3:6 | *Seek [the Lord's] will in all you do, and he will show you which path to take.*

PROVERBS 16:6 | *Unfailing love and faithfulness make atonement for sin. By fearing the LORD, people avoid evil.*

PROVERBS 16:17 | *The path of the virtuous leads away from evil; whoever follows that path is safe.*

ROMANS 13:14 | *Clothe yourself with the presence of the Lord Jesus Christ. And don't let yourself think about ways to indulge your evil desires.*

Keeping a close relationship with God is the most important way to avoid those things you need to avoid. Just as staying close to a fire on a cold night keeps you warm, staying close to God in a dangerous world protects you from spiritual attack and keeps you from drifting back into old habits of sin. Seek daily wisdom from God and you will avoid many temptations, bad habits, and mistakes in judgment.

What follows is a topical guide to several specific things you should try to avoid as you walk the road to recovery.

ANGER/HATRED

How can I control my anger?

PROVERBS 29:11 | *Fools vent their anger, but the wise quietly hold it back.*

EPHESIANS 4:26 | *"Don't sin by letting anger control you." Don't let the sun go down while you are still angry.*

1 PETER 2:21, 23 | *God called you to do good, even if it means suffering, just as Christ suffered for you. He is your example, and you must follow in his steps. . . . He did not retaliate when he was insulted, nor threaten revenge when he suffered. He left his case in the hands of God, who always judges fairly.*

Anger is dangerous because it can take away your inhibitions. Do you ever remember being angry and then doing something you shouldn't have because you just didn't care at the moment? Anger can make you not care about the consequences of your actions. If you want to recover, then you must not let anger control your actions. Instead, focus on your freedom to make a choice to control your anger when it rises up in you.

PSALM 4:4 | *Don't sin by letting anger control you. Think about it overnight and remain silent.*

PROVERBS 19:11 | *Sensible people control their temper; they earn respect by overlooking wrongs.*

In order to not let anger control you, think through an issue ahead of time and plan a way to prevent yourself from giving in to anger. You will remember this when the issue threatens to make you angry, and it will be easier to keep yourself from letting it consume you.

PSALM 37:8 | *Stop being angry! Turn from your rage! Do not lose your temper—it only leads to harm.*

EPHESIANS 4:31-32 | *Get rid of all bitterness, rage, anger, harsh words, and slander, as well as all types of evil behavior. Instead, be kind to each other, tenderhearted, forgiving one another, just as God through Christ has forgiven you.*

Train yourself to examine your heart whenever you become angry. Ask yourself, *Who is really offended in this situation? Is this about God's honor or my pride? Am I acting with humility or out of revenge?* Questions like these will help you to figure out why you are angry, which helps you focus on letting go of the anger and being loving instead.

How do I let go of hatred?

GENESIS 37:5 | *One night Joseph had a dream, and when he told his brothers about it, they hated him more than ever.*

COLOSSIANS 3:8, 13 | *Now is the time to get rid of anger [and] rage. . . . Make allowance for each other's faults, and forgive anyone who offends you. Remember, the Lord forgave you, so you must forgive others.*

When you hate others, it is hard to even consider forgiving them. This makes your heart cold and hard, allowing bitterness to affect all you say and do.

MATTHEW 5:43-44 | *[Jesus said,] "You have heard the law that says, 'Love your neighbor' and hate your enemy. But I say, love your enemies! Pray for those who persecute you!"*

1 JOHN 4:20 | *If someone says, "I love God," but hates a Christian brother or sister, that person is a liar; for if we don't love people we can see, how can we love God, whom we cannot see?*

When you love God, you learn to let go of hatred because you learn to love everyone else. God made all people, and he calls you to love them too. They experience the same problems and challenges you do, and they long for the same happiness. Love them and forgive them if they have wronged you—and then watch hatred leave your life. Once hatred is gone, recovery will be easier. In fact, you cannot recover as long as you harbor hatred and bitterness in your heart.

APATHY

What happens if apathy is allowed to grow in my life?

JEREMIAH 7:26 | *[The Lord said,] "My people have not listened to me or even tried to hear."*

COLOSSIANS 1:23 | *You must continue to believe this truth and stand firmly in it. Don't drift away from the assurance you received when you heard the Good News.*

REVELATION 3:15-16 | *[God said,] "I know all the things you do, that you are neither hot nor cold. I wish that you were one or the other! But since you are like lukewarm water, neither hot nor cold, I will spit you out of my mouth!"*

If you become apathetic—meaning you don't care much about anything anymore—then everything about your life will start to go downhill. This will eventually make it difficult to want to keep living. Interestingly, you still hurt inside when you are apathetic because you really wish your life were happy and fulfilling. In order to make this a reality, you must start to care. Ask God to give you the motivation to change, and he will. God has promised his joy to his people.

ASSUMPTIONS

What are some assumptions I should avoid?

ROMANS 5:8-9, 11 | *God showed his great love for us by sending Christ to die for us while we were still sinners. And since we have been made right in God's sight by the blood of Christ, he will certainly save us from God's condemnation. . . . So now we can rejoice in our wonderful new relationship with God because our Lord Jesus Christ has made us friends of God.*

Don't assume God doesn't care, for the Bible clearly shows he does.

JUDGES 6:13-14 | *"Sir," Gideon [said], "if the LORD is with us, why has all this happened to us? And where are all the miracles our ancestors told us about? Didn't they say, 'The LORD brought us up out of Egypt'? But now the LORD has abandoned us and handed us over to the Midianites." Then the LORD turned to him and said, "Go with the strength you have, and rescue Israel from the Midianites. I am sending you!"*

Don't assume God won't help you or doesn't want to help you, for he has already done so in more ways than you know, and he will continue to do so. And don't assume you know the way through your problems better than God does.

JOHN 14:6 | *Jesus [said], "I am the way, the truth, and the life. No one can come to the Father except through me."*

Don't just assume you will go to heaven. The Bible says the only way to heaven is by accepting Jesus Christ as Savior and Lord.

JOHN 3:8 | *Just as you can hear the wind but can't tell where it comes from or where it is going, so you can't explain how people are born of the Spirit.*

ACTS 16:27-30 | *The jailer woke up to see the prison doors wide open. He assumed the prisoners had escaped, so he drew his sword to kill himself. But Paul shouted to him, "Stop! Don't kill yourself! We are all here!" The jailer called for lights and ran to the dungeon and fell down trembling before Paul and Silas. Then he brought them out and asked, "Sirs, what must I do to be saved?"*

Don't assume that someone won't respond to the good news of Jesus. In God's hands, people can be transformed into godly heroes.

ACTS 9:13, 15 | *"But Lord," exclaimed Ananias, "I've heard many people talk about the terrible things this man has done to the believers in Jerusalem!" . . . But the Lord said, "Go, for Saul is my chosen instrument to take my message to the Gentiles and to kings, as well as to the people of Israel."*

Don't assume people can't change. Like Paul (previously known as Saul), even the worst sinner can become a great Christian leader.

1 CHRONICLES 19:2-3 | *David said, "I am going to show loyalty to Hanun because his father, Nahash, was always loyal to me." So David sent messengers to express sympathy to Hanun about his father's death. But when David's ambassadors arrived in the land of Ammon, the Ammonite commanders said to Hanun, "Do you really think these men are coming here to honor your father? No! David has sent them to spy out the land so they can come in and conquer it!"*

Don't assume the worst in others; you may miss out when they want to give their best to you.

BACKSLIDING

What do I do when I've fallen away from God?

PSALM 32:5 | *Finally, I confessed all my sins to you and stopped trying to hide my guilt. I said to myself, "I will confess my rebellion to the LORD." And you forgave me! All my guilt is gone.*

AMOS 5:4 | *This is what the LORD says . . .: "Come back to me and live!"*

ROMANS 3:23-24 | *Everyone has sinned; we all fall short of God's glorious standard. Yet God, with undeserved kindness, declares that we are righteous. He did this through Christ Jesus when he freed us from the penalty for our sins.*

1 JOHN 1:9 | *If we confess our sins to him, he is faithful and just to forgive us our sins and to cleanse us.*

Backsliding will probably happen to you from time to time, as it does to almost everyone. You'll suddenly realize you are further from God than you should be. It worries you, maybe scares you. Don't ignore that warning. Find out what happened—was it simple neglect, or more likely, was it a sinful habit that you didn't want to give up? Only when you recognize what you've done can you confess it to God, and only by confessing can you be forgiven and begin the process of restoring your relationship with him. Confessing is a verbal expression that you want to move back toward him. It is the act of acknowledging that your sin has separated you from God. God's forgiving you is the act of bringing you back into fellowship.

BITTERNESS

What are the signs of bitterness?

1 SAMUEL 18:8 | *Saul [became] very angry. "What's this?" he said. "They credit David with ten thousands and me with only thousands. Next they'll be making him their king!"*

Anger. Anger allowed to fester and grow will always turn into bitterness.

GENESIS 42:36 | *Jacob exclaimed, "You are robbing me of my children! Joseph is gone! Simeon is gone! And now you want to take Benjamin, too. Everything is going against me!"*

Grief. Prolonged grief that has turned to despair will cause you to look at life as meaningless, and you will feel bitter.

GENESIS 31:1 | *Jacob . . . learned that Laban's sons were grumbling about him. "Jacob has robbed our father of everything!" they said. "He has gained all his wealth at our father's expense."*

Resentment. Resentment causes you to look at others' success with suspicion. This creates a bitter spirit.

ACTS 6:1 | *As the believers rapidly multiplied, there were rumblings of discontent. The Greek-speaking believers complained about the Hebrew-speaking believers, saying that their widows were being discriminated against in the daily distribution of food.*

Discontentment. Discontentment is rooted in jealousy, which causes you to think you aren't getting what you deserve. When the focus shifts to you and what you aren't getting, bitterness sets in.

NUMBERS 12:1-2 | *Miriam and Aaron criticized Moses because he had married a Cushite woman. They said, "Has the LORD spoken only through Moses? Hasn't he spoken through us, too?" But the LORD heard them.*

A critical spirit. If you often find wrong in others, then you are in danger of letting bitterness control your life.

GENESIS 30:15 | *Leah angrily replied [to Rachel], "Wasn't it enough that you stole my husband? Now will you steal my son's mandrakes, too?"*

Jealousy. Jealousy leads to anger. Unresolved anger leads to bitterness. Allowed to grow, bitterness can lead to harmful behavior toward those you envy.

How do I deal with my bitterness toward others?

MARK 11:25 | *When you are praying, first forgive anyone you are holding a grudge against, so that your Father in heaven will forgive your sins, too.*

2 CORINTHIANS 2:7 | *It is time to forgive and comfort him. Otherwise he may be overcome by discouragement.*

EPHESIANS 4:31-32 | *Get rid of all bitterness. . . . Instead, be kind to each other, tenderhearted, forgiving one another, just as God through Christ has forgiven you.*

Forgiveness is the antidote to bitterness. It lifts burdens, cancels debts, and frees you from the chains of unresolved anger.

PHILIPPIANS 1:12 | *[Paul said,] "I want you to know, my dear brothers and sisters, that everything that has happened to me here has helped to spread the Good News."*

Paul was traveling the world sharing the good news about Jesus. Then he was thrown into prison for sharing his faith. That could have made him bitter; instead, he saw it as an opportunity. He knew that God takes even the worst situations and, if we allow him to, he brings good out of them. Paul couldn't wait to see the good that God would bring out of his prison time. It was while in prison that Paul wrote many of the New Testament letters, which have brought countless millions to faith in Jesus. That's a lot of good out of a bad situation! God is waiting for you to let him do the same in your difficult situations.

BOREDOM

Isn't being a Christian boring?

PROVERBS 26:14 | *As a door swings back and forth on its hinges, so the lazy person turns over in bed.*

ECCLESIASTES 2:23 | *Their days of labor are filled with pain and grief; even at night their minds cannot rest. It is all meaningless.*

GALATIANS 6:9 | *Let's not get tired of doing what is good. At just the right time we will reap a harvest of blessing if we don't give up.*

Getting tired of what is good, experiencing a sense of meaninglessness, feeling lazy—these are all signs of boredom. It is important to recognize the signs and to persist in doing good in spite of them.

HEBREWS 6:11-12 | *Our great desire is that you will keep on loving others as long as life lasts, in order to make certain that what you hope for will come true. Then you will not become spiritually dull and indifferent.*

Being a Christian can seem boring to many—"Don't do this," "You can't do that." But those who grasp what the Christian life is all about find it full and exciting. When you realize that almighty God wants to work through you to accomplish some of his work in the world, you will be amazed to see the great things he will do through you. Focus on using and developing your God-given gifts as well as on the eternal rewards God promises to believers, and your life will be continually exciting. If you become bored in your Christian life, it is because you are not making yourself available to God so he can pour his blessings through you to others.

COMPARISONS

What are the dangers of comparing myself to others?

2 CORINTHIANS 10:12 | *Oh, don't worry; we wouldn't dare say that we are as wonderful as these other men who tell you how important they are! But they are only comparing themselves with each other, using themselves as the standard of measurement. How ignorant!*

Comparing yourself to someone else is foolish because it usually leads to sinful thoughts. If you think you're better than someone, you'll be proud, and pride is a dangerous sin. If you think you're not as good as someone else, you'll tend to become jealous, and jealousy is a sin that can lead to anger and to behavior that is hurtful to others.

JOHN 21:21-22 | *Peter asked Jesus, "What about him, Lord?" Jesus replied, "If I want him to remain alive until I return, what is that to you? As for you, follow me."*

Comparing yourself to someone else takes your focus off Jesus.

LUKE 18:11-14 | *The Pharisee stood by himself and prayed this prayer: "I thank you, God, that I am not a sinner like everyone else. For I don't cheat, I don't sin, and I don't commit adultery. I'm certainly not like that tax collector! I fast twice a week, and I give you a tenth of my income." But the tax collector stood at a distance and dared not even lift his eyes to heaven as he prayed. Instead, he beat his chest in sorrow, saying, "O God, be merciful to me, for I am a sinner." I tell you, this sinner, not the Pharisee, returned home justified*

*before God. For those who exalt themselves will be humbled,
and those who humble themselves will be exalted.*

Comparing the condition of your heart to that of someone
else can lead to false righteousness, thinking you are better
than others, and pride. On the flip side, thinking you are
far worse than others can lead to deep shame, discouragement, and despair. God knows the condition of your heart,
and he loves you as you are. Keep focused on him and you
won't have a need to compare.

1 CORINTHIANS 12:18-22, 26-27 | *Our bodies have many parts, and
God has put each part just where he wants it. How strange
a body would be if it had only one part! Yes, there are many
parts, but only one body. The eye can never say to the hand,
"I don't need you." The head can't say to the feet, "I don't need
you." In fact, some parts of the body that seem weakest and
least important are actually the most necessary. . . . If one part
suffers, all the parts suffer with it, and if one part is honored,
all the parts are glad. All of you together are Christ's body,
and each of you is a part of it.*

If you were asked to get rid of one part of your body, it
might be difficult to choose. Your left leg? Your right arm?
Your nose? Eye? Thumb? Some parts are more attractive
than others, but they are all important to help you live and
function as effectively as possible. In the same way, God
created every person with a specific function in mind, a
definite role to serve in his Kingdom. Comparisons serve
only to trivialize someone's function. When you build
others up and seek unity, it enhances everyone's function
in the body of Christ.

DECEPTION

Why is deception so harmful?

PSALM 101:7 | *I will not allow deceivers to serve in my house, and liars will not stay in my presence.*

MARK 7:20-23 | *It is what comes from inside that defiles you. For from within, out of a person's heart, come evil thoughts . . . deceit. . . . These vile things come from within; they are what defile you.*

Honesty is the opposite of deceit. God wants you to be completely honest in your life because that is the only way to have a good reputation and be a good example of Christian living. When you are honest in all the details of your life, you experience the distinct advantages of having a clear conscience and earning the trust and respect of others, as well as receiving God's blessing. You can build a good reputation by consistent, honest behavior, and you can start today.

How does deceiving others hurt me?

EPHESIANS 4:25 | *Stop telling lies. Let us tell our neighbors the truth, for we are all parts of the same body.*

When you lie to someone, you chip away at the foundation of truth and trust that is absolutely essential to a healthy relationship. Furthermore, you cannot introduce deceit into any relationship without opening the door to allow Satan, "the father of lies" (see John 8:44), to take a foothold and tempt you to deceive even more.

DESIRES

How do I know if my desires are right or wrong?

JUDGES 14:3 | *[Samson's] father and mother objected. "Isn't there even one woman in our tribe or among all the Israelites you could marry?" they asked. "Why must you go to the pagan Philistines to find a wife?" But Samson told his father, "Get her for me! She looks good to me."*

Selfish desires take only yourself into account. You become so obsessed with what you want that you forget to ask if it is what God would want, if it's actually good for you, or if it would harm others.

ROMANS 6:12 | *Do not let sin control the way you live; do not give in to sinful desires.*

1 CORINTHIANS 3:3 | *You are still controlled by your sinful nature. You are jealous of one another and quarrel with each other. Doesn't that prove you are controlled by your sinful nature? Aren't you living like people of the world?*

PHILIPPIANS 4:8 | *Fix your thoughts on what is true, and honorable, and right, and pure, and lovely, and admirable. Think about things that are excellent and worthy of praise.*

Desiring sin is always wrong. Make sure that the object of your desire is good, that it is consistent with God's Word, and that it is not harmful to others.

How do wrong desires grow in me?

JAMES 4:2-3 | *You want what you don't have, so you scheme and kill to get it. You are jealous of what others have, but you can't get it, so you fight and wage war to take it away from them. Yet you don't have what you want because you don't ask God for it. And even when you ask, you don't get it because your motives are all wrong—you want only what will give you pleasure.*

A seed is planted, quietly, without fanfare or drums, without malice or evil intent—you simply take a step away from God. With the second and third steps, you move further from God, and the bitter, poisonous fruit of wrong desires grows until you cannot control it.

How can I resist harmful desires?

JAMES 3:13 | *If you are wise and understand God's ways, prove it by living an honorable life, doing good works with the humility that comes from wisdom.*

Keep yourself busy with good deeds.

MATTHEW 6:13 | *Don't let us yield to temptation, but rescue us from the evil one.*

Pray that good desires will overcome bad ones.

2 CHRONICLES 34:33 | *Josiah removed all detestable idols . . . and throughout the rest of his lifetime, [the people] did not turn away from the LORD.*

Get rid of the source of temptation.

COLOSSIANS 3:2 | *Think about the things of heaven.*

Fill your mind with God and thoughts that honor him.

PROVERBS 15:22 | *Plans go wrong for lack of advice; many advisers bring success.*

Find a person willing to help you. People need someone who will encourage them and hold them accountable.

Can God help me change the desires of my heart? How?

EZEKIEL 36:26 | *[The sovereign Lord said,] "I will give you a new heart, and I will put a new spirit in you. I will take out your stony, stubborn heart and give you a tender, responsive heart."*

2 CORINTHIANS 5:17 | *Anyone who belongs to Christ has become a new person. The old life is gone; a new life has begun!*

When you give control of your life to God, he gives you a new heart, a new nature, and a new desire to please him.

EZRA 1:5 | *God stirred the hearts of the priests and Levites . . . to rebuild the Temple of the LORD.*

God stirs your heart with right desires. It is up to you to act upon them.

DISHONESTY

How is dishonesty hurtful in relationships?

ROMANS 13:9-10 | *The commandments say, "You must not commit adultery. You must not murder. You must not steal. You must not covet." These—and other such commandments—are summed up in this one commandment: "Love your neighbor as yourself." Love does no wrong to others, so love fulfills the requirements of God's law.*

Dishonesty is inconsistent with a loving relationship. Who can trust a cheating heart?

GENESIS 27:12 | *[My father will] see that I'm trying to trick him, and then he'll curse me instead of blessing me.*

HABAKKUK 2:9-10 | *What sorrow awaits you who build big houses with money gained dishonestly! You believe your wealth will buy security, putting your family's nest beyond the reach of danger. But by the murders you committed, you have shamed your name and forfeited your lives.*

Dishonesty results in fear and shame. You live in fear that you will be discovered and that your character will be revealed.

PROVERBS 20:23 | *The LORD detests double standards; he is not pleased by dishonest scales.*

Dishonesty causes you to be untrustworthy and untrusting. Dishonesty eventually makes you unable to relate to others. Double standards are no standards at all.

1 SAMUEL 15:13, 17, 19-20, 24 | *Saul greeted [Samuel] cheerfully. "May the LORD bless you," he said. "I have carried out the LORD's command!" . . . And Samuel [asked] him . . . "Why haven't you obeyed the LORD? Why did you rush for the plunder and do what was evil in the LORD's sight?" "But I did obey the LORD," Saul insisted. . . . Then Saul admitted to Samuel, "Yes, I have sinned. I have disobeyed your instructions and the LORD's command, for I was afraid of the people and did what they demanded."*

Dishonesty can begin to seem like truth over time. By believing your own lies, you deceive yourself, alienate yourself from God, and lose credibility in your relationships. When you deceive yourself, you have lost all hope of finding the truth.

What are the consequences of dishonesty?

JOSHUA 9:3-6, 16, 22 | *When the people of Gibeon heard what Joshua had done to Jericho and Ai, they resorted to deception to save themselves. They sent ambassadors to Joshua, loading their donkeys with weathered saddlebags and old, patched wineskins. They put on worn-out, patched sandals and ragged clothes. And the bread they took with them was dry and moldy. When they arrived at the camp of Israel at Gilgal, they told Joshua and the men of Israel, "We have come from a distant land to ask you to make a peace treaty with us.". . . Three days after making the treaty, they learned that these people actually lived nearby! . . . Joshua called together the Gibeonites and said, "Why did you lie to us? Why did you say that you live in a distant land when you live right here among us?"*

PROVERBS 12:19 | *Truthful words stand the test of time, but lies are soon exposed.*

Dishonesty is usually exposed in one way or another. Dishonesty can ruin your reputation of being worthy of trust; cause you to lose your friends, your spouse, your home, or your job; and in some cases, cause you to land in jail. But ultimately, a pattern of dishonesty pits you against the God of truth, who won't allow dishonest people into his eternal Kingdom. That is why few things are more important than practicing honesty.

DISOBEDIENCE

How should I respond to areas of disobedience in my life?

EXODUS 32:21-24 | *[Moses] turned to Aaron and demanded, "What did these people do to you to make you bring such terrible sin upon them?" "Don't get so upset, my lord," Aaron replied. ". . . They said to me, 'Make us gods who will lead us. We don't know what happened to this fellow Moses, who brought us here from the land of Egypt.' So I told them, 'Whoever has gold jewelry, take it off.' When they brought it to me, I simply threw it into the fire—and out came this calf!"*

Excusing sin is never an appropriate response. When you try to excuse your sin, you just compound it.

PSALM 51:1-4 | *Have mercy on me, O God, because of your unfailing love. Because of your great compassion, blot out the stain of my sins. Wash me clean from my guilt. Purify me from my sin. For I recognize my rebellion; it haunts me day and night. Against you, and you alone, have I sinned; I have done what is evil in your sight. You will be proved right in what you say, and your judgment against me is just.*

1 JOHN 1:9 | *If we confess our sins to him, he is faithful and just to forgive us our sins and to cleanse us.*

Confessing that you have sinned is always the appropriate response to areas of disobedience in your life.

DEUTERONOMY 10:12-13 | *What does the LORD your God require of you? He requires only that you fear the LORD your God, and live in a way that pleases him, and love him and serve him with all your heart and soul. And you must always obey the LORD's commands.*

ROMANS 4:7 | *Oh, what joy for those whose disobedience is forgiven, whose sins are put out of sight.*

Joyfully accept God's forgiveness; then commit yourself to obeying him.

DRINKING

Is it wrong for Christians to drink alcohol?

ROMANS 14:21 | *It is better not to eat meat or drink wine or do anything else if it might cause another believer to stumble.*

EPHESIANS 5:18 | *Don't be drunk with wine, because that will ruin your life. Instead, be filled with the Holy Spirit.*

The Bible does not say that having a drink is wrong, but it clearly says that being drunk is. The difference between having a drink and drinking is the control factor. Drinking becomes a problem when you become drunk or lose control of what you say or do after you drink. Any drinking that impairs your thinking or your behavior is wrong. When needing a drink dominates your thoughts or dictates your schedule or when drinking becomes an essential or necessary part of your day, then you have lost control to the power of alcohol. The Bible teaches that self-control is one of the ingredients of right living, and when you sacrifice self-control for self-indulgence, you are sacrificing your safety, your reputation, your family and friends, and your relationship with

God. Drinking should be avoided for almost anyone on the
road to recovery—you have enough things in your life trying
to control you, so you don't need one more.

When does drinking become wrong?

EXODUS 32:6 | *The people got up early the next morning to
sacrifice burnt offerings and peace offerings. After this, they
celebrated with feasting and drinking, and they indulged in
pagan revelry.*

PROVERBS 23:29-32 | *Who has anguish? Who has sorrow? Who is
always fighting? Who is always complaining? Who has unneces-
sary bruises? Who has bloodshot eyes? It is the one who spends
long hours in the taverns, trying out new drinks. Don't gaze at
the wine, seeing how red it is, how it sparkles in the cup, how
smoothly it goes down. For in the end it bites like a poisonous
snake; it stings like a viper.*

LUKE 21:34 | *Watch out! Don't let your hearts be dulled by
carousing and drunkenness.*

Drinking becomes wrong when it leads to drunkenness,
when it influences your thoughts or actions, or when it
causes you to disobey and dishonor God.

EVIL

Why does evil exist?

DANIEL 7:25 | *He will defy the Most High and oppress the holy
people of the Most High. He will try to change their sacred*

festivals and laws, and they will be placed under his control for a time.

Satan's evil purpose is to wear down believers until they are led into sin. This gives Satan pleasure and greater power on the earth.

Where does evil come from?

EZEKIEL 28:12-17 | *[The Sovereign Lord said,] "You were the model of perfection. . . . You were in Eden, the garden of God. . . . I ordained and anointed you as the mighty angelic guardian. . . . You were blameless in all you did from the day you were created until the day evil was found in you . . . and you sinned. So I banished you in disgrace. . . . I expelled you, O mighty guardian. . . . I threw you to the ground."*

Evil began in the heart of Satan, once a mighty angel warrior in heaven. When he sinned against God, he was expelled from heaven and now roams the earth causing people to sin. This is the root cause of your addictions and troubles, from which you need recovery and healing.

ROMANS 3:23 | *Everyone has sinned; we all fall short of God's glorious standard.*

ROMANS 7:18-23 | *[Paul said,] "I know that nothing good lives in me, that is, in my sinful nature. I want to do what is right, but I can't. I want to do what is good, but I don't. I don't want to do what is wrong, but I do it anyway. But if I do what I don't want to do, I am not really the one doing wrong; it is sin living in me that does it. I have discovered this principle of life—that when I want to do what is right, I inevitably do what is wrong. I love God's law with all my heart. But there is another power within me that is at war with my mind. This power makes me a slave to the sin that is still within me."*

Ever since Satan first convinced Adam and Eve to sin, everyone has been born with a sinful nature (see Romans 5:12). All people are all literally born with a spiritual disease that causes them to sin—the desire to go their own way instead of God's way. The proof of this is that no one has ever lived a perfect life except Jesus, God's Son. So while you can work to sin less and to keep sin from controlling you, you can never—on this earth—eliminate sin altogether.

JEREMIAH 17:9 I *The human heart is the most deceitful of all things, and desperately wicked. Who really knows how bad it is?*

Your own heart, polluted by sin and selfishness, becomes a source for evil thoughts and actions.

EPHESIANS 6:12 I *We are not fighting against flesh-and-blood enemies, but against evil rulers and authorities of the unseen world, against mighty powers in this dark world, and against evil spirits in the heavenly places.*

Cosmic forces of evil, led by Satan, are engaged in a deadly rebellion against God and against you personally if you claim allegiance to God.

How can I combat and confront evil?

EPHESIANS 6:16 I *Hold up the shield of faith to stop the fiery arrows of the devil.*

1 JOHN 4:4 I *You belong to God, my dear children. You have already won a victory over those [false prophets], because the*

Spirit who lives in you is greater than the spirit who lives in the world.

1 JOHN 5:4 | *Every child of God defeats this evil world, and we achieve this victory through our faith.*

Your first line of defense is to draw strength from the fact that God is more powerful than your problems and your enemies. Your faith in God is like a shield that protects you from the temptations and criticisms hurled at you every day. Without strong faith, the weapons of Satan and the arrows shot at you by your enemies would pierce and defeat you. So when life seems overwhelming, hold tightly to your faith like a shield and you will withstand the dangers and discouragements Satan sends you. And rejoice, knowing that God has already won the victory.

ROMANS 12:9 | *Don't just pretend to love others. Really love them. Hate what is wrong. Hold tightly to what is good.*

Resolve to hate everything that is sinful and evil.

1 CORINTHIANS 10:12-13 | *If you think you are standing strong, be careful not to fall. The temptations in your life are no different from what others experience. And God is faithful. He will not allow the temptation to be more than you can stand. When you are tempted, he will show you a way out so that you can endure.*

Stop giving in to temptation. God's Word makes it clear that sin always hurts you because it separates you from God (your source of mercy and blessing) and puts you in the clutches of the enemy. Giving in to temptation puts you in the middle of a road with evil hurtling toward you at high speed, and being run over by sin and its consequences will cause great distress in your life. The next time you find yourself in the way of sin, get off the road of temptation before its consequences run you over. God has promised to give you the strength to resist.

ROMANS 13:14 | *Clothe yourself with the presence of the Lord Jesus Christ. And don't let yourself think about ways to indulge your evil desires.*

Make sure you don't put yourself in situations where you know your resolve for righteousness will be tested. The closer you walk with Christ, the harder it is to be caught in the snare of evil.

ROMANS 12:21 | *Don't let evil conquer you, but conquer evil by doing good.*

Combat evil with goodness. This is a difficult thing to do, but ultimately, it is the only thing that will work, for God's goodness is stronger than evil.

MATTHEW 4:5-7 | *The devil took [Jesus] to the holy city, Jerusalem, to the highest point of the Temple, and said, "If you are the Son of God, jump off! For the Scriptures say, 'He will order his angels to protect you. And they will hold you up with their hands so you won't even hurt your foot on a stone.'" Jesus responded, "The Scriptures also say, 'You must not test the LORD your God.'"*

JAMES 4:7 | *Humble yourselves before God. Resist the devil, and he will flee from you.*

The devil has less power than you think. The devil can tempt you, but he cannot coerce you. You can resist the devil as Jesus did—by responding to the lies of temptation with the truth of God's Word.

1 JOHN 4:4 | *The Spirit who lives in you is greater than the spirit who lives in the world.*

You must never forget that God's Holy Spirit is great enough to overcome any threat against you.

FEAR

What can I do when I am overcome with fear?

PSALM 46:1-2 | *God is our refuge and strength, always ready to help in times of trouble. So we will not fear when earthquakes come and the mountains crumble into the sea.*

Know that God is greater than the most severe happenings in life. You will not be surprised or overwhelmed by trouble if you recognize how sin has corrupted this world and if you walk close to God each day. He promises to always be ready to help you when you ask.

JOHN 14:27 | *[Jesus said,] "I am leaving you with a gift—peace of mind and heart. And the peace I give is a gift the world cannot give. So don't be troubled or afraid."*

Believe that God's Son, Jesus, promises to comfort you and give you the assurance that he is with you in any circumstance.

DEUTERONOMY 31:6 | *Be strong and courageous! Do not be afraid and do not panic. . . . For the LORD your God will personally go ahead of you. He will neither fail you nor abandon you.*

Remind yourself that God is always with you. Your situation may be genuinely threatening, but God has not abandoned you and he promises to stay with you. Even if your situation is so bad that it results in death, God has not left you but has instead ushered you into his very presence.

EPHESIANS 1:3 | *All praise to God, the Father of our Lord Jesus Christ, who has blessed us with every spiritual blessing in the heavenly realms because we are united with Christ.*

Remind yourself that no enemy or adversity can take away your most important blessings—the forgiveness God gave you for your sins, your relationship with him, and your eternal salvation. These remain secure even when your world falls apart.

PHILIPPIANS 4:6-7 | *Don't worry about anything; instead, pray about everything. Tell God what you need, and thank him for all he has done. Then you will experience God's peace, which exceeds anything we can understand. His peace will guard your hearts and minds as you live in Christ Jesus.*

Pray with a thankful heart, asking God to give you what you need to deal with your fear. Peace is not the absence of fear, but the conquest of fear. Peace is not running away, but overcoming.

GENESIS 26:7, 10 | *When the men who lived there asked Isaac about his wife, Rebekah, he said, "She is my sister." He was afraid to say, "She is my wife." He thought, "They will kill me to get her, because she is so beautiful." . . . "How could you do this to us?" Abimelech exclaimed. "One of my people might easily have taken your wife and slept with her, and you would have made us guilty of great sin."*

JOSHUA 17:16 | *The Canaanites . . . have iron chariots. . . . They are too strong for us.*

You are not meant to live in fear, but sometimes you may find yourself in a fearful situation. Fear must not keep you from doing the things you know are right.

GUILT

How do I handle lingering feelings of guilt, even after I have confessed my sin?

ACTS 10:36 | *This is the message of Good News . . . that there is peace with God through Jesus Christ, who is Lord of all.*

ACTS 13:39 | *Everyone who believes in [Jesus] is declared right with God—something the law of Moses could never do.*

ROMANS 1:16-17 | *I am not ashamed of this Good News about Christ. It is the power of God at work, saving everyone who believes—the Jew first and also the Gentile. This Good News tells us how God makes us right in his sight. This is accomplished from start to finish by faith. As the Scriptures say, "It is through faith that a righteous person has life."*

Sometimes it is hard to believe news that seems too good to be true. God's good news is the best news you'll ever hear, and best of all, it *is* true! Every person is on death row—doomed to an eternity of being separated from God. All people have been declared "guilty." Escape might seem impossible, especially if you have done some terrible things, but God offers the most amazing gift to everyone—freedom from eternal death and then life forever in heaven with him where all is perfect and good. And all you have to do is believe it by accepting the truth that Jesus died for your sins. When you do, your guilt is gone completely and your life is changed. You'll gratefully follow Jesus and live the way he asks his believers to live because anyone who can free you from a death sentence is worth following. God doesn't want you to feel guilty about being free; he wants you to enjoy your freedom and make the most of it.

HABITS

How can God help me deal with bad habits?

ROMANS 7:15 | *[Paul said,] "I don't really understand myself, for I want to do what is right, but I don't do it. Instead, I do what I hate."*

One of the best ways to deal with bad habits is to recognize them for what they are and confess them honestly. Paul knew that he could not kick the habit of sin completely. But he also knew that, with God's help, he could make progress every day. In the same way, you may have to give up a habit in phases, one step at a time.

ROMANS 8:5-6 | *Those who are dominated by the sinful nature think about sinful things, but those who are controlled by the Holy Spirit think about things that please the Spirit. So letting your sinful nature control your mind leads to death. But letting the Spirit control your mind leads to life and peace.*

God has given you the Holy Spirit to help make you holy. While victory does not always come immediately, you will progress as you submit your mind and heart to the love, wisdom, and truth of God's Spirit living in you.

ROMANS 6:12-14 | *Do not let sin control the way you live; do not give in to sinful desires. Do not let any part of your body become an instrument of evil to serve sin. Instead, give yourselves completely to God, for you were dead, but now you have new life. So use your whole body as an instrument to do what is right for the glory of God. Sin is no longer your master, for you no longer live under the requirements of the law. Instead, you live under the freedom of God's grace.*

One of Satan's great lies is that you are a victim, with no power to resist some of the strong influences around you. The world teaches you that heredity, environment, and circumstances excuse you from responsibility. But God is more powerful than anything that seeks to control you. When you call upon his power through prayer and the support of the Holy Spirit and fellow believers, God breaks the chains that hold you and sets you free.

GENESIS 2:16-17; 3:6 | *The LORD God warned [the man], "You may freely eat the fruit of every tree in the garden—except the tree of the knowledge of good and evil." . . . The woman . . . saw that the tree was beautiful and its fruit looked delicious. . . . So she took some of the fruit and ate it. Then she gave some to her husband, who was with her, and he ate it, too.*

1 JOHN 2:15 | *Do not love this world nor the things it offers you, for when you love the world, you do not have the love of the Father in you.*

Sin often appears lovely and attractive. In the same way, indulging in bad habits often feels good even though you know these habits are ultimately bad for you. Breaking a bad habit can be hard because you are losing something you enjoy. But understand that losing a bad habit ultimately brings a deeper satisfaction from doing what is pleasing to God.

ROMANS 8:5 I *Those who are dominated by the sinful nature think about sinful things, but those who are controlled by the Holy Spirit think about things that please the Spirit.*

COLOSSIANS 3:2 I *Think about the things of heaven, not the things of earth.*

It will be much easier to break bad habits if you replace them with good habits.

HIDING YOUR SINS

How do I find the courage to stop hiding my sins?

PSALM 142:1-3 I *I cry out to the LORD; I plead for the LORD's mercy. I pour out my complaints before him and tell him all my troubles. When I am overwhelmed, you alone know the way I should turn.*

JEREMIAH 23:24 I *"Can anyone hide from me in a secret place? Am I not everywhere in all the heavens and earth?" says the LORD.*

Go to God honestly, realizing that you are not revealing any new information to him. Your courage begins when you admit that you need someone's help, and who can help you more than God? Go to him first, and he may reveal others who can help you as well.

PSALM 32:5, 7 | *Finally, I confessed all my sins to you and stopped trying to hide my guilt. I said to myself, "I will confess my rebellion to the LORD." And you forgave me! All my guilt is gone. . . . You are my hiding place; you protect me from trouble. You surround me with songs of victory.*

PROVERBS 28:13 | *People who conceal their sins will not prosper, but if they confess and turn from them, they will receive mercy.*

Confessing your sins brings them out of hiding so they can be forgiven and forgotten forever by God.

PSALM 19:12 | *How can I know all the sins lurking in my heart? Cleanse me from these hidden faults.*

PSALM 119:105 | *Your word is a lamp to guide my feet and a light for my path.*

HEBREWS 4:12 | *The word of God is alive and powerful. It is sharper than the sharpest two-edged sword, cutting between soul and spirit, between joint and marrow. It exposes our innermost thoughts and desires.*

Look to God's Word, asking God to reveal what needs to be exposed. God's Word shines a light on the sins lurking in the dark corners of your life. Only when you stop hiding your sins can you be released from their power to control you.

JOSHUA 7:13 | *Get up! Command the people to purify themselves in preparation for tomorrow. For this is what the LORD, the God of Israel, says: Hidden among you, O Israel, are things set apart for the LORD. You will never defeat your enemies until you remove these things from among you.*

1 SAMUEL 10:20-24 | *Samuel brought all the tribes of Israel before the LORD, and the tribe of Benjamin was chosen by lot. Then he brought each family of the tribe of Benjamin before the LORD, and the family of the Matrites was chosen. And finally Saul son of Kish was chosen from among them. But when they looked for him, he had disappeared! So they asked the LORD, "Where is he?" And the LORD replied, "He is hiding among the baggage." So they found him and brought him out, and he stood head and shoulders above anyone else. Then Samuel said to all the people, "This is the man the LORD has chosen as your king. No one in all Israel is like him!"*

Sometimes you are forced out of hiding to face either your punishment or your reward. Sins, confessed or unconfessed, may still bring consequences. Goodness, recognized or unrecognized, will bring blessings.

HOPELESSNESS

What can hopelessness lead to?

PSALM 143:4 | *I am losing all hope; I am paralyzed with fear.*

Hopelessness can paralyze you with fear, and fear produces only more hopelessness.

JOB 6:11 | *I don't have the strength to endure. I have nothing to live for.*

Hopelessness drains your strength and cripples your endurance, which produces only more hopelessness.

ECCLESIASTES 2:17 | *I came to hate life because everything done here under the sun is so troubling. Everything is meaningless—like chasing the wind.*

Hopelessness can lead to bitterness, driving a wedge between you and those who could encourage you.

ECCLESIASTES 9:3 | *It seems so tragic that everyone under the sun suffers the same fate. That is why people are not more careful to be good. Instead, they choose their own mad course, for they have no hope. There is nothing ahead but death anyway.*

ISAIAH 22:13 | *You dance and play; you slaughter cattle and kill sheep. You feast on meat and drink wine. You say, "Let's feast and drink, for tomorrow we die!"*

Hopelessness can prompt self-indulgence, with its ever-increasing appetite for more, which produces an ever-increasing hopelessness that "I don't have enough."

PSALM 88:15-18 | *I have been sick and close to death since my youth. I stand helpless and desperate before your terrors. Your fierce anger has overwhelmed me. Your terrors have paralyzed me. They swirl around me like floodwaters all day long. They have engulfed me completely. You have taken away my companions and loved ones. Darkness is my closest friend.*

PROVERBS 13:12 | *Hope deferred makes the heart sick, but a dream fulfilled is a tree of life.*

1 THESSALONIANS 4:13 | *We want you to know what will happen to the believers who have died so you will not grieve like people who have no hope.*

Hopelessness leads to despair, which makes you want to give up.

1 KINGS 19:4 | *[Elijah] went on alone into the wilderness, traveling all day. He sat down under a solitary broom tree and prayed that he might die. "I have had enough, LORD," he said. "Take my life, for I am no better than my ancestors who have already died."*

ECCLESIASTES 4:1-2 | *I observed all the oppression that takes place under the sun. I saw the tears of the oppressed, with no one to comfort them. The oppressors have great power, and their victims are helpless. So I concluded that the dead are better off than the living.*

JONAH 4:3, 8 | *"Just kill me now, LORD! I'd rather be dead than alive if what I predicted will not happen." . . . And as the sun grew hot, God arranged for a scorching east wind to blow on Jonah. The sun beat down on his head until he grew faint and wished to die. "Death is certainly better than living like this!" he exclaimed.*

MATTHEW 27:5 | *Judas threw the silver coins down in the Temple and went out and hanged himself.*

Hopelessness can make you feel worthless, perhaps even to the point of having thoughts of suicide.

What can I do when I feel hopeless?

PSALM 33:22 | *Let your unfailing love surround us, LORD, for our hope is in you alone.*

PSALM 42:5-6 | *Why am I discouraged? Why is my heart so sad? I will put my hope in God! I will praise him again—my Savior and my God! Now I am deeply discouraged, but I will remember you.*

Remember what God has done for you and begin to praise him, even if it's for something small. The more you do this, the more will come to mind to praise him for, and your hope will begin to grow.

LAZINESS

Is it wrong to be lazy?

PROVERBS 21:25 | *Despite their desires, the lazy will come to ruin, for their hands refuse to work.*

PROVERBS 24:30-34 | *I walked by the field of a lazy person. . . . I saw that it was overgrown . . . and its walls were broken down. . . . I learned this lesson: A little extra sleep, a little more slumber, a little folding of the hands to rest—then poverty will pounce on you like a bandit.*

Laziness is considered one of the "seven deadly sins" but is often considered to be not that bad. People tend to think of sin as doing something they shouldn't, but it is also neglecting to do what they should. Laziness is a sin because it wastes your God-given talents and ability to work, wastes the time God has given you on earth, and wastes opportunities to serve God and others. Laziness selfishly expects others to provide for you and opens the door to temptation with your idle time. It can be transformed by purpose. Having a purpose requires courage and discipline to say no to those distractions that contribute to laziness. Another point to note is that laziness is not the same as rest. Laziness is a waste of time and energy, whereas rest rejuvenates the body and soul.

How can I overcome laziness?

PSALM 37:30-31 | *The godly offer good counsel; they teach right from wrong. They have made God's law their own, so they will never slip from his path.*

PROVERBS 12:15 | *Fools think their own way is right, but the wise listen to others.*

PROVERBS 27:9 | *The heartfelt counsel of a friend is as sweet as perfume and incense.*

If you have a habit of being lazy, or if others accuse you of being lazy, there may be other issues that are the root cause of it. You may be dealing with depression, or there may be a medical reason. Seek help from a counselor and a doctor. God has given you special abilities and spiritual gifts, and most people truly want to live a life of purpose. If you just can't get going, it helps to rule out a psychological or medical reason for your lack of energy and motivation—listen to those who can help you.

PRETENDING

What are the dangers/consequences of pretending to be what I am not?

PSALM 101:7 | *I will not allow deceivers to serve in my house, and liars will not stay in my presence.*

PROVERBS 20:23 | *The LORD detests double standards; he is not pleased by dishonest scales.*

PROVERBS 21:27 | *The sacrifice of an evil person is detestable, especially when it is offered with wrong motives.*

MARK 12:38, 40 | *Jesus . . . taught: "Beware of these teachers of religious law! For they . . . shamelessly cheat widows out of their property and then pretend to be pious by making long prayers in public. Because of this, they will be more severely punished."*

1 PETER 2:1-3 | *Get rid of all evil behavior. Be done with all deceit, hypocrisy, jealousy, and all unkind speech. Like newborn babies, you must crave pure spiritual milk so that you will grow into a full experience of salvation. Cry out for this nourishment, now that you have had a taste of the Lord's kindness.*

God is opposed to pretending (also known as hypocrisy) because it shows a heart of dishonesty. Much of pretending grows out of deceit, which is harmful to your spiritual growth. When you pretend, you deceive others into thinking you are something you really are not.

PSALM 25:3 | *No one who trusts in you will ever be disgraced, but disgrace comes to those who try to deceive others.*

Pretending eventually leads to disgrace. You risk shame when you are exposed.

MICAH 6:12 | *The rich among you have become wealthy through extortion and violence. Your citizens are so used to lying that their tongues can no longer tell the truth.*

1 TIMOTHY 4:2 | *These people are hypocrites and liars, and their consciences are dead.*

After a while, pretending based on deceit becomes a habit and even acceptable, dulling and even deadening your conscience. Eventually deceivers deceive themselves, cutting themselves off from truth.

PROCRASTINATION

Why do I procrastinate? And is it really so bad?

PROVERBS 6:10-11 | *A little extra sleep, a little more slumber, a little folding of the hands to rest—then poverty will pounce on you like a bandit; scarcity will attack you like an armed robber.*

Procrastination is often a form of laziness, which the Bible calls sin.

JONAH 1:3 | *But Jonah got up and went in the opposite direction to get away from the LORD.*

Fear of the cost of obeying God can paralyze you or cause you to run from God and waste the very resources and talents he has given you. Don't put off or run away from doing what you know God wants you to do.

MATTHEW 25:25 | *I was afraid I would lose your money, so I hid it in the earth.*

Fear of failure can make you not want to start a task. It's better to try and fail a couple of times than to never try at all.

PSALM 143:7 | *Come quickly, LORD, and answer me, for my depression deepens. Don't turn away from me, or I will die.*

Depression is often a cause of procrastination. In the midst of depression, it is difficult to do anything.

LUKE 8:13 | *The seeds on the rocky soil represent those who hear the message and receive it with joy. But since they don't have deep roots, they believe for a while, then they fall away when they face temptation.*

1 THESSALONIANS 3:5 | *That is why, when I could bear it no longer, I sent Timothy to find out whether your faith was still strong. I was afraid that the tempter had gotten the best of you and that our work had been useless.*

Temptation can cause you to procrastinate because Satan's strategy is to distract you from doing the work God assigns you.

QUITTING

How can I keep going when I feel like quitting?

NEHEMIAH 4:2-3 | *What does this bunch of poor, feeble Jews think they're doing? . . . That stone wall would collapse if even a fox walked along the top of it!*

Faced with an overwhelming task and ridicule from adversaries, Nehemiah kept his eyes on his goal and his call. Like Nehemiah, you can resist quitting by keeping focused on your goals.

ACTS 20:22-24 | *[Paul said,] "I am bound by the Spirit to go to Jerusalem. I don't know what awaits me, except that the Holy Spirit tells me in city after city that jail and suffering lie ahead.*

But my life is worth nothing to me unless I use it for finishing the work assigned me by the Lord Jesus—the work of telling others the Good News about the wonderful grace of God."

Paul faced unimaginable hardship yet never gave up, finishing the work to which God had called him. If you believe the Holy Spirit has called you to do something, let his power and encouragement keep you from quitting when the going gets tough.

2 CORINTHIANS 4:8-9 | *We are pressed on every side by troubles, but we are not crushed. We are perplexed, but not driven to despair. We are hunted down, but never abandoned by God. We get knocked down, but we are not destroyed.*

Even in the midst of suffering, believers can find strength from Jesus to endure.

MATTHEW 10:22 | *Everyone who endures to the end will be saved.*

GALATIANS 6:9 | *Let's not get tired of doing what is good. At just the right time we will reap a harvest of blessing if we don't give up.*

2 TIMOTHY 4:7 | *I have fought the good fight, I have finished the race, and I have remained faithful.*

You can avoid discouragement and the desire to quit by keeping your eyes on the goal of finishing well and on the reward of heaven. Even during times when suffering or difficulties seem never ending, having an eternal perspective (knowing you'll spend eternity with Jesus in heaven) gives you hope by reminding you that these times are only temporary and that one day there will be no more pain or suffering (see Revelation 21:4).

ACTS 14:22 | *They encouraged [the believers] to continue in the faith, reminding them that we must suffer many hardships to enter the Kingdom of God.*

REVELATION 2:3 | *You have patiently suffered for me without quitting.*

Endurance is an antidote to quitting. When you continue to obey God's Word even in difficult times, you demonstrate that your faith is strong. When you refuse to get discouraged and give up, God rewards your endurance. Trusting God means that you confidently expect him to guide you through each day until you see him face-to-face.

ECCLESIASTES 10:4 | *If your boss is angry at you, don't quit! A quiet spirit can overcome even great mistakes.*

Quitting gives a person the reputation of being unreliable and untrustworthy. Be faithful in whatever you do, for when you can be trusted with small things, you have a better chance of being trusted with larger responsibilities. Even in the face of criticism, continue to work hard and display a cheerful spirit. Others will notice, and your reputation will be enhanced.

2 CORINTHIANS 4:8, 14, 16 | *We are pressed on every side by troubles, but we are not crushed. We are perplexed, but not driven to despair. . . . We know that God, who raised the Lord Jesus, will also raise us with Jesus and present us to himself together with you. . . . That is why we never give up.*

When God has called you to a task and you give up, you miss the great blessings of reaching your goal and of trusting God to help you get there. Just because God is in something doesn't make it easy. In fact, the harder the road, the stronger you become. If you know God is leading you and opening doors in a certain direction, don't give up just because the going gets tough. If anything, that should tell you that you are headed in the right direction. Keep moving forward boldly and with faith.

REGRETS

How can I deal with the regrets of my life?

2 CORINTHIANS 5:17 | *Anyone who belongs to Christ has become a new person. The old life is gone; a new life has begun!*

When you come to faith in Jesus, he forgives your sins—all of them. Your past is forgotten by him, and he gives you a fresh start. You will still have to live with the consequences of your sins because they cannot be retracted. But because God forgives you, you can move forward without the tremendous guilt that can accompany regret.

MICAH 7:19 | *Once again you will have compassion on us. You will trample our sins under your feet and throw them into the depths of the ocean!*

Because God no longer holds your sins against you, you no longer have to hold them against yourself. Now you can be free from self-condemnation.

PSALM 51:1-3, 17 | *Have mercy on me, O God, because of your unfailing love. Because of your great compassion, blot out the stain of my sins. Wash me clean from my guilt. Purify me from my sin. For I recognize my rebellion; it haunts me day and night. . . . The sacrifice you desire is a broken spirit. You will not reject a broken and repentant heart, O God.*

PSALM 119:75 | *I know, O LORD, that your regulations are fair; you disciplined me because I needed it.*

Ask yourself if God may be communicating something through your regrets. God sometimes uses brokenness and remorse to bring spiritual insight and growth. Regrets that drive you to God are redemptive.

PHILIPPIANS 3:13 | *I focus on this one thing: Forgetting the past and looking forward to what lies ahead.*

Focus on God, who controls the future, not on regrets of the past. The past is over, so don't live a "what if" life of regret, feeling angry at yourself for what you did and bitter toward God for allowing you to do it. God doesn't cause regrets; he washes them away when you ask him to walk with you into the future.

MATTHEW 16:18 | *[Jesus said,] "Now I say to you that you are Peter (which means 'rock'), and upon this rock I will build my church, and all the powers of hell will not conquer it."*

MATTHEW 26:69-75 | *A servant girl came over and said to [Peter], "You were one of those with Jesus the Galilean." But Peter denied it in front of everyone. "I don't know what you're talking about," he said. Later, out by the gate, another servant girl noticed him and said to those standing around, "This man was with Jesus of Nazareth." Again Peter denied it, this time with an oath. "I don't even know the man," he said. A little later some of the other bystanders came over to Peter and said, "You must be one of them; we can tell by your Galilean accent."*

Peter swore, "A curse on me if I'm lying—I don't know the man!" And immediately the rooster crowed. Suddenly, Jesus' words flashed through Peter's mind: "Before the rooster crows, you will deny three times that you even know me." And he went away, weeping bitterly.

GALATIANS 2:7-9 | *God had given . . . Peter the responsibility of preaching to the Jews. . . . God . . . worked through Peter as the apostle to the Jews. . . . In fact, James, Peter, and John . . . were known as pillars of the church.*

Turn your regrets into resolve. Regrets can be so powerful that they disable you from serving God in the future. If Peter had focused on his regret over denying Jesus, he would never have been able to preach the good news about Jesus so powerfully. Don't let regret paralyze you; instead, let it motivate you to positive action for God.

PSALM 30:11 | *You have turned my mourning into joyful dancing. You have taken away my clothes of mourning and clothed me with joy.*

PHILIPPIANS 4:6 | *Don't worry about anything; instead, pray about everything. Tell God what you need, and thank him for all he has done.*

God wants to take your burdens from you and to restore your relationship with him and with others. Don't cause the biggest regret of your life—withdrawing from God. No matter what you've done, he welcomes you with loving arms.

ROMANS 8:28 | *We know that God causes everything to work together for the good of those who love God and are called according to his purpose for them.*

Remember that God has the ability to turn bad into good. He can use even the things you regret to accomplish his will.

MATTHEW 18:21-22 | *Peter . . . asked, "Lord, how often should I forgive someone who sins against me? Seven times?" "No, not seven times," Jesus replied, "but seventy times seven!"*

LUKE 15:18 | *I will go home to my father and say, "Father, I have sinned against both heaven and you."*

ROMANS 4:6-8 | *David . . . described the happiness of those who are declared righteous without working for it: "Oh, what joy for those whose disobedience is forgiven, whose sins are put out of sight. Yes, what joy for those whose record the LORD has cleared of sin."*

Sin always brings regret because it damages the relationships most important to you. Sometimes it is your own sin that has caused the problem, and sometimes it is the sin of others against you. In either case, the sin has caused a deep rift in the relationship and now you are facing conflict, separation, loneliness, frustration, anger, and other emotions. Confessing your sin to God and others, asking for forgiveness, gives your heart a chance to start over. And forgiving others of their sin against you gives you the chance for a fresh start. Forgiveness is the glue that holds friendship together. It doesn't take away the regret, but it changes your perspective from regret to restoration. It keeps you focused on the healing that can happen in the future rather than on the wounds that you received in the past.

RESPECT FOR AUTHORITY

What if I have a bad attitude toward authority?

ROMANS 13:7 | *Pay your taxes and government fees to those who collect them, and give respect and honor to those who are in authority.*

HEBREWS 3:7-10 | *The Holy Spirit says, "Today when you hear his voice, don't harden your hearts as Israel did when they rebelled, when they tested me in the wilderness. There your ancestors tested and tried my patience, even though they saw my miracles for forty years. So I was angry with them, and I said, 'Their hearts always turn away from me. They refuse to do what I tell them.'"*

Sometimes being told what to do is unpleasant: You want to chart your own course and become your own person. But being your own person and being rebellious are two totally different things. Authority is not always a bad thing; the abuse of authority is what is bad. God's authority—his rules—will not only save your life but will show you how to be successful and blessed. Don't rebel against that authority, because you jeopardize your very soul. Being your own person doesn't mean doing whatever you want to; it means using your God-given personality and talents to serve him through serving others.

MATTHEW 20:26 | *Whoever wants to be a leader among you must be your servant.*

JOHN 3:30 | *[John said,] "[The Messiah] must become greater and greater, and I must become less and less."*

If you want to be looked up to by others, then have a servant's heart, be willing to take responsibility for your actions (not passing the buck), refuse to stay silent when things are wrong, and do not constantly seek glory for yourself. The world has taught you to look and act cool, to use coarse or foul language, to not respect authority, and to bend the rules as far as you can. But in the end, it's the people who have consistently lived with kindness, integrity, and a deep love for God who will be most respected and honored.

SEXUAL SIN

If I'm single, how can I practice abstinence? How do I develop self-control?

PROVERBS 25:28 | *A person without self-control is like a city with broken-down walls.*

1 PETER 1:13 | *Think clearly and exercise self-control. Look forward to the gracious salvation that will come to you when Jesus Christ is revealed to the world.*

2 PETER 1:5-6 | *Supplement your faith with a generous provision of moral excellence, and moral excellence with knowledge, and knowledge with self-control, and self-control with patient endurance, and patient endurance with godliness.*

Self-control is a key to abstinence, and it comes from allowing God's Spirit within you to help you think clearly and make right choices. When you think clearly, it becomes easier to make better choices and you become motivated to choose the right way. When your choices are better, your actions are easier to control.

GENESIS 39:6-7, 10-12 | *Joseph was a very handsome and well-built young man, and Potiphar's wife soon began to look at him lustfully. "Come and sleep with me," she demanded. . . . She kept putting pressure on Joseph day after day, but he refused to sleep with her, and he kept out of her way as much as possible. One day, however, no one else was around when he went in to do his work. She came and grabbed him by his cloak, demanding, "Come on, sleep with me!" Joseph tore himself away, but he left his cloak in her hand as he ran from the house.*

PROVERBS 4:15 | *Don't even think about it; don't go that way. Turn away and keep moving.*

AMOS 5:14 | *Do what is good and run from evil so that you may live! Then the LORD God of Heaven's Armies will be your helper.*

1 CORINTHIANS 6:18 | *Run from sexual sin! No other sin so clearly affects the body as this one does. For sexual immorality is a sin against your own body.*

1 TIMOTHY 6:11 | *You, Timothy, are a man of God; so run from all these evil things.*

There are times when the best way to practice abstinence is to physically remove yourself from a tempting situation. It is hard to do this when your thoughts are telling you to stay, but only because you are dwelling on it. If you leave a tempting situation immediately, it will become easier each time.

How do I protect myself from getting into an adulterous relationship?

MATTHEW 15:19 | *From the heart come evil thoughts, . . . adultery, all sexual immorality, [and] lying.*

The seeds of adultery are planted in the garden of the heart. Guard what is planted there—through what you read, watch, and think about—to avoid growing the fruit of adultery.

PROVERBS 2:16 | *Wisdom will save you from the immoral woman, from the seductive words of the promiscuous woman.*

JAMES 1:5 | *If you need wisdom, ask our generous God, and he will give it to you. He will not rebuke you for asking.*

God promises wisdom to those who ask him for it. Wisdom will give you the discernment to know how to avoid adultery. You still must make the choice to avoid it, but wisdom helps you recognize the early warning signs that you are moving in the wrong direction.

PROVERBS 4:25-27 | *Look straight ahead, and fix your eyes on what lies before you. Mark out a straight path for your feet; stay on the safe path. Don't get sidetracked; keep your feet from following evil.*

If looking can lead you into adultery, then not looking will help you avoid it. It can be challenging to have "faithful eyes," but this is a key to success in avoiding adultery.

PROVERBS 5:3-4, 8-9 | *The lips of an immoral woman are as sweet as honey, and her mouth is smoother than oil. But in the end she is as bitter as poison. . . . Stay away from her! Don't go near the door of her house! If you do, you will lose your honor and will lose to merciless people all you have achieved.*

When faced with temptation, you might think that you can handle it, but the most effective course is to run away and not look back—to avoid tempting situations whenever possible.

PROVERBS 5:15, 18 I *Drink water from your own well—share your love only with your wife. . . . Let your wife be a fountain of blessing for you. Rejoice in the wife of your youth.*

Adultery is more likely to happen if you allow discontentment to creep into your heart. You won't be tempted to "shop around" when you are content with your mate and consciously rejoice over the blessing he or she is to you.

SIN

How can I be free from sin's guilt and power?

ISAIAH 1:18 I *"Come now, let's settle this," says the LORD. "Though your sins are like scarlet, I will make them as white as snow. Though they are red like crimson, I will make them as white as wool."*

ROMANS 5:1-2 I *Since we have been made right in God's sight by faith, we have peace with God because of what Jesus Christ our Lord has done for us. Because of our faith, Christ has brought us into this place of undeserved privilege where we now stand, and we confidently and joyfully look forward to sharing God's glory.*

ROMANS 5:6, 9-11 I *When we were utterly helpless, Christ came at just the right time and died for us sinners. . . . And since we have been made right in God's sight by the blood of Christ, he will certainly save us from God's condemnation. For since our friendship with God was restored by the death of his Son while we were still his enemies, we will certainly be saved through the life of his Son. So now we can rejoice in our wonderful new relationship with God because our Lord Jesus Christ has made us friends of God.*

COLOSSIANS 1:21-22 | *You . . . were once far away from God. You were his enemies, separated from him by your evil thoughts and actions. Yet now he has reconciled you to himself through the death of Christ in his physical body.*

God has made it possible for the stain of your sin to be removed through the death and resurrection of Jesus Christ.

PSALM 19:12 | *How can I know all the sins lurking in my heart? Cleanse me from these hidden faults.*

PSALM 51:2-3 | *Wash me clean from my guilt. Purify me from my sin. For I recognize my rebellion; it haunts me day and night.*

PSALM 139:23-24 | *Search me, O God, and know my heart; test me and know my anxious thoughts. Point out anything in me that offends you, and lead me along the path of everlasting life.*

1 JOHN 1:9 | *If we confess our sins to him, he is faithful and just to forgive us our sins and to cleanse us.*

Ask God to cleanse your heart from sin so that it is open and ready for his Holy Spirit to enter. Confessing your sins to God, turning away from them to obey him, is the only way to be free from sin's power and your guilt. When you confess your sins to God, he forgives you and forgets your sin.

ROMANS 6:6-9, 18 | *Our old sinful selves were crucified with Christ so that sin might lose its power in our lives. We are no longer slaves to sin. For when we died with Christ we were set free from the power of sin. And since we died with Christ, we know we will also live with him. We are sure of this because Christ was raised from the dead, and he will never die again. Death no longer has any power over him. . . . Now you are free from your slavery to sin, and you have become slaves to righteous living.*

Because of Jesus' death and resurrection, when you confess your sins and believe in Jesus as the Son of God, you are free from the power of sin. This doesn't mean you will no longer sin but that sin's power to enslave you has been defeated.

Am I really a Christian if I still sin?

JOHN 16:33 | *[Jesus said,] "I have told you all this so that you may have peace in me. Here on earth you will have many trials and sorrows. But take heart, because I have overcome the world."*

ROMANS 7:20 | *[Paul said,] "If I do what I don't want to do, I am not really the one doing wrong; it is sin living in me that does it."*

GALATIANS 5:17 | *The sinful nature wants to do evil, which is just the opposite of what the Spirit wants. And the Spirit gives us desires that are the opposite of what the sinful nature desires. These two forces are constantly fighting each other.*

You will always struggle with sin, but once you have placed your faith in Jesus, he guarantees victory over it.

ROMANS 8:5 | *Those who are dominated by the sinful nature think about sinful things, but those who are controlled by the Holy Spirit think about things that please the Spirit.*

Sin loses its influence over you as you increasingly yield your life to the control of the Holy Spirit. The Spirit of God living in you reduces your appetite for sin and increases your hunger for God.

PSALM 119:11 | *I have hidden your word in my heart, that I might not sin against you.*

The Bible leads you away from sin, for it contains the words from a holy God to guide you along the path that is best for you.

SPIRITUAL DRYNESS

What happens if spiritual dryness continues in my life?

ISAIAH 32:12-13 | *Beat your breasts in sorrow for your bountiful farms and your fruitful grapevines. For your land will be over-grown with thorns and briers. Your joyful homes and happy towns will be gone.*

JEREMIAH 12:4 | *How long must this land mourn? Even the grass in the fields has withered. The wild animals and birds have disappeared because of the evil in the land.*

Your life will become empty and withered.

JEREMIAH 2:19 | *Your wickedness will bring its own punishment. Your turning from me will shame you. You will see what an evil, bitter thing it is to abandon the* LORD *your God and not to fear him. I, the Lord, the* LORD *of Heaven's Armies, have spoken!*

JEREMIAH 7:26 | *[The Lord said,] "My people have not listened to me or even tried to hear. They have been stubborn and sinful."*

JEREMIAH 36:24 | *Neither the king nor his attendants showed any signs of fear or repentance at [Jeremiah's messages from the Lord].*

EZEKIEL 12:2 | *[The Lord said,] "Son of man, you live among rebels who have eyes but refuse to see. They have ears but refuse to hear. For they are a rebellious people."*

EZEKIEL 20:8 | *[The Lord said,] "They rebelled against me and would not listen. They did not get rid of the vile images they were obsessed with, or forsake the idols of Egypt. Then I threatened to pour out my fury on them to satisfy my anger while they were still in Egypt."*

Spiritual dryness can lead to a life of rebellious, sinful living.

JEREMIAH 7:24 | *[The Lord said,] "My people would not listen to me. They kept doing whatever they wanted, following the stubborn desires of their evil hearts. They went backward instead of forward."*

MATTHEW 12:30 | *[Jesus said,] "Anyone who isn't with me opposes me, and anyone who isn't working with me is actually working against me."*

HEBREWS 2:3 | *What makes us think we can escape if we ignore this great salvation that was first announced by the Lord Jesus himself and then delivered to us by those who heard him speak?*

REVELATION 3:15-16 | *[God said,] "I know all the things you do, that you are neither hot nor cold. I wish that you were one or the other! But since you are like lukewarm water, neither hot nor cold, I will spit you out of my mouth!"*

It is not possible to put God on hold. There is no standing still in your relationship with him. You are either moving closer to him or moving away from him. Apathy about your relationship with God withers your soul.

TEMPTATION

How can I avoid giving in to temptation or peer pressure?

GENESIS 3:6 | *The woman . . . saw that the tree was beautiful and its fruit looked delicious, and she wanted the wisdom it would give her. So she took some of the fruit and ate it.*

1 KINGS 11:1, 3 | *King Solomon loved many foreign women. . . . And in fact, they did turn his heart away from the LORD.*

If sin weren't attractive, you wouldn't have a problem with it. Recognize that this is how Satan will try to tempt you. It is the only way he has to make you do what is not right. Although both sin and right living leave you wanting more, sin will never fulfill you, whereas right living will. Focus on God's way of living, doing what is right. This will leave you happier and more fulfilled than sin ever could.

GENESIS 39:10 | *[Potiphar's wife] kept putting pressure on Joseph day after day, but he refused to sleep with her, and he kept out of her way as much as possible.*

EXODUS 23:2 | *You must not follow the crowd in doing wrong. When you are called to testify in a dispute, do not be swayed by the crowd to twist justice.*

PSALM 1:1 | *Oh, the joys of those who do not follow the advice of the wicked, or stand around with sinners, or join in with mockers.*

PROVERBS 1:10 | *If sinners entice you, turn your back on them!*

PROVERBS 14:7 | *Stay away from fools, for you won't find knowledge on their lips.*

1 CORINTHIANS 15:33 | *Don't be fooled by those who say such things, for "bad company corrupts good character."*

Perhaps the most obvious way to avoid negative peer pressure is to choose wise peers. If your friends constantly persuade you to do wrong, you might need to stay away from them until you have the strength to resist their temptations.

MATTHEW 14:9 | *The king regretted what he had said; but because of the vow he had made in front of his guests, he issued the necessary orders.*

JAMES 4:17 | *Remember, it is sin to know what you ought to do and then not do it.*

Pride and embarrassment are poor reasons for your choices. Can you remember a good situation coming out of letting your pride or potential embarrassment make the decision? Never let these feelings influence your decisions because the consequences are always bad. Always.

PSALM 101:4 | *I will reject perverse ideas and stay away from every evil.*

ISAIAH 8:11 | *The LORD has given me a strong warning not to think like everyone else does.*

Remember that agreeing with what everyone else thinks is not always right. The crowd doesn't necessarily move in the right direction. An example of this is the media. How many times has media—television, magazines, and so forth—reported something as "fact," then later admitted to new facts? If you seek God's wisdom, you will stay true to what is right and avoid what is wrong.

1 CORINTHIANS 10:13 | *The temptations in your life are no different from what others experience. And God is faithful. He will not allow the temptation to be more than you can stand. When you are tempted, he will show you a way out so that you can endure.*

Remind yourself that when temptation might become so strong you can't handle it, God has made a way of escape for you. Realizing this every time someone pressures you to do something wrong will help you remember that there is a way out of it for the asking.

DANIEL 1:8 | *Daniel was determined not to defile himself by eating the food and wine given to [him] by the king. He asked the chief of staff for permission not to eat these unacceptable foods.*

A solid commitment made before temptation strikes is the best prevention to sin. Temptation has less power over you if you have already determined that you will not yield to it. Think about all the reasons why you should resist a specific sin if it comes your way again, and then make up your mind to not let the sin control you.

MATTHEW 6:9, 13 | *Pray like this: . . . Don't let us yield to temptation, but rescue us from the evil one.*

Make your need to resist temptation a constant focus of prayer. God will recognize your true desire to stop giving in to the sin if you ask him for his help.

ECCLESIASTES 4:12 | *A person standing alone can be attacked and defeated, but two can stand back-to-back and conquer. Three are even better, for a triple-braided cord is not easily broken.*

Friends are people who care about you. If you simply ask them to question you periodically about your specific sin, they will do so because they do not want you to keep going down the road that is so obviously hurting you.

1 JOHN 4:4 | *The Spirit who lives in you is greater than the spirit who lives in the world.*

1 JOHN 5:4-5 | *Every child of God defeats this evil world, and we achieve this victory through our faith. And who can win this battle against the world? Only those who believe that Jesus is the Son of God.*

If you have been giving in to a controlling sin for a while, your mind is not thinking the way it should. You can break free from temptation when you change your focus and train your mind. Instead of thinking about your weakness, fill your mind with the promise of God's strength. Instead of thinking about what you're missing out on, think about what you'll be gaining by moving in a different direction. You have far more power available to you than you are aware of.

WEAKNESSES/VULNERABILITIES I 209

How do I guard and protect my heart?

PROVERBS 4:23 I *Guard your heart above all else, for it determines the course of your life.*

PROVERBS 23:19 I *My child, listen and be wise: Keep your heart on the right course.*

1 JOHN 5:21 I *Keep away from anything that might take God's place in your hearts.*

The intent of a guardrail on a dangerous curve is not to inhibit your freedom to drive, but to save your life! That guardrail is a sign of security and safety, not an obstacle! In the same way, you need a "guardrail" as you travel through life, not to inhibit your freedom but to keep your life from going out of control. Your heart determines where you go because it is the center for your passions and emotions. If you don't guard your heart with God's Word and stay focused on the road God wants you to travel, you may have a terrible accident when temptation distracts you.

WEAKNESSES/VULNERABILITIES

How can my weaknesses defeat me?

JUDGES 16:15-17 I *Delilah pouted, "How can you tell me, 'I love you,' when you don't share your secrets with me?" . . . She tormented him with her nagging day after day until he was sick to death of it. Finally, Samson shared his secret with her.*

ROMANS 6:12 I *Do not let sin control the way you live; do not give in to sinful desires.*

3 JOHN 1:11 | *Dear friend, don't let [a] bad example influence you. Follow only what is good.*

The crafty Philistines knew they couldn't match Samson's brute strength, so they aimed at his weakness—his inability to stay away from seductive women. Temptation always strikes at your weak spot. "How can you say you love me?" Delilah whined, and Samson gave in. Your weak spots are those areas you refuse to give over to God. They are joints in your spiritual armor at which the enemy takes aim, the areas in which you compromise your convictions for pleasure or other temporal gain. It is in those areas of weakness that you must ask God for help so he can cover your vulnerable spots with his strength. You must understand your weaknesses so you can arm yourself against Satan's attacks. It is a disaster to discover your weak spots in the heat of the battle; you must discover them before the fighting begins. With a strategy in place to protect your points of vulnerability, you will be prepared for the enemy's attacks.

Part Six

Traits Needed to Recover

HUMILITY . . . to first of all recognize that I have a problem and admit to myself what it is.

ATTITUDE . . . to believe I can change and overcome my problem.

PERSPECTIVE . . . to look differently at my problem, to no longer see change as impossible but as possible.

PRAYER . . . to submit to God as the Power who can help me, to admit to him my problem, and to thank him for continuing to love me in spite of my problem.

MOTIVES . . . to really want to change now.

CONVICTIONS . . . to determine the way I really want to live and what I must do to achieve that.

SURRENDER . . . to be completely willing to give up my own way of doing things and truly desire to follow God's way of doing things.

HOPE . . . to really believe that I can do this, that recovery is possible, and that a new way of living for God will bring long-term joy.

FAITH . . . to know that God wants to heal me and to trust that God is going to be with me every step of the way in my recovery journey.

COURAGE . . . *to get started in fighting my problem and/or addiction.*

VISION . . . *to make a plan to recover, imagining myself recovered down the road and beginning to see how to get there.*

MOTIVATION . . . *to develop specific ideas that can encourage me to keep going in the right direction.*

SELF-CONTROL . . . *to develop the discipline to keep following the plan once it goes into action and to find someone who will keep me accountable to stay on course.*

CONFIDENCE . . . *to trust that the plan will work.*

TRUST . . . *to believe that God will help the plan to work.*

PATIENCE . . . *to accept that it will take time for full recovery to happen.*

ENDURANCE . . . *to keep at it and never give up so that the goal will be reached.*

THANKFULNESS . . . *to God and others for a new lease on life and the victories along the way.*

STABILITY . . . *to not give in to impulsive urges and to keep moving forward one step at a time.*

RESPONSIBILITY . . . *to follow my plan and to make decisions (after getting input from others) that show I am serious about my recovery.*

POTENTIAL . . . *to have faith that I can become all God created me to be.*

HUMILITY

—————————————————————•●

. . . to first of all recognize that I have a problem and admit to myself what it is.

Why is humility so important to recovery?

DANIEL 10:12 | *[The man in the vision] said, "Don't be afraid, Daniel. Since the first day you began to pray for understanding and to humble yourself before your God, your request has been heard in heaven. I have come in answer to your prayer."*

1 PETER 5:6-7 | *Humble yourselves under the mighty power of God, and at the right time he will lift you up in honor. Give all your worries and cares to God, for he cares about you.*

Humility is the wisdom and courage to admit your needs. You won't get help—from God or others—until you can admit that you have a problem. Pride keeps you from admitting your problem; humility is the first step toward resolving it.

ISAIAH 29:19 | *The humble will be filled with fresh joy from the LORD. The poor will rejoice in the Holy One of Israel.*

ISAIAH 57:15 | *The high and lofty one who lives in eternity, the Holy One, says this: . . . "I restore the crushed spirit of the humble."*

When you turn to God in humility, you admit that you need help to change and that you believe you've found the greatest source of help. God promises refreshment and fulfillment if you humble yourself. Once you give your problems over to him, he will help you begin your road to recovery.

ATTITUDE

◂◦

. . . to believe I can change and overcome my problem.

How does my attitude affect my recovery?

ROMANS 8:6 | *Letting your sinful nature control your mind leads to death. But letting the Spirit control your mind leads to life and peace.*

ROMANS 14:17 | *The Kingdom of God is not a matter of what we eat or drink, but of living a life of goodness and peace and joy in the Holy Spirit.*

In order to start recovering, you must change your viewpoint about the things that are controlling you—addictions, bad habits, lifestyle choices—and the way you look at them. Things that control you tend to be comforting, even when they are bad for you. You must ask God's Holy Spirit to fill your heart and mind. He gives you the positive attitude you need to change, to help you see what he really wants you to become. Then the road to recovery will look a lot more attractive and worthwhile.

How can a positive attitude carry me through hard times?

ROMANS 8:17-18 | *Since we are [God's] children, we are his heirs. In fact, together with Christ we are heirs of God's glory. But if we are to share his glory, we must also share his suffering. Yet what we suffer now is nothing compared to the glory he will reveal to us later.*

PHILIPPIANS 4:11-13 | *I have learned how to be content with whatever I have. I know how to live on almost nothing or with everything. I have learned the secret of living in every situation, whether it is with a full stomach or empty, with plenty or little. For I can do everything through Christ, who gives me strength.*

1 THESSALONIANS 5:18 | *Be thankful in all circumstances, for this is God's will for you who belong to Christ Jesus.*

Hard times and life struggles are the raw materials for God's mighty work in your life. While it is hard to be thankful *for* the tough times, you can be thankful *in* them. Your outlook on life determines how you view your problems. If you see them only as obstacles, you will probably develop an attitude of bitterness, cynicism, and hopelessness. If you see your problems as a crucible for strengthening your character and convictions, you will be able to rise above them and even thank God for how they are refining your life.

PERSPECTIVE

. . . to look differently at my problem, to no longer see change as impossible but possible.

How did I lose perspective?

NUMBERS 17:12-13 | *The people of Israel said to Moses, "Look, we are doomed! We are dead! We are ruined! Everyone who even comes close to the Tabernacle of the LORD dies. Are we all doomed to die?"*

JONAH 1:1-3 | *The LORD gave this message to Jonah son of Amittai: "Get up and go to the great city of Nineveh." . . . But Jonah got up and went in the opposite direction to get away from the LORD.*

In the story from the book of Numbers, the perspective of the people was completely opposite to reality. Instead of seeing the Tabernacle as a place to *go to* because of God's presence there, they saw it as a place to *avoid* because of God's presence. Instead of seeing God as the One who gives life, they saw him as someone who threatens death. What happened? Their perspective of God changed because their daily choices changed from deciding to do things God's way to deciding not to do things his way. This is not to say that you deliberately reject God every time you disobey him, but when your perspective on life is different from God's, you naturally lose sight of what is important in life. God is the One to *go to* in times of trouble, not to ignore or run away from. The prophet Jonah learned this valuable lesson the hard way.

What are the blessings of seeing things from God's perspective?

PSALM 138:8 | *The LORD will work out his plans for my life.*

PSALM 139:3 | *You see me when I travel and when I rest at home. You know everything I do.*

ROMANS 12:2 | *Don't copy the behavior and customs of this world, but let God transform you into a new person by changing the way you think. Then you will learn to know God's will for you, which is good and pleasing and perfect.*

Wouldn't it be nice to have the perspective of seeing the world the way its Creator sees it? You will someday discover that your life is like a tapestry. Now you can see only sections of the back, with many knots and loose ends. Someday you will see the front in its beautiful entirety, the picture of world history and your personal history from God's perspective. If you could see unexpected and even unwelcome circumstances in this way, you'll embrace both the good and the bad, knowing they are creating a beautiful picture God is weaving with your life. As you give God control, his perspectives will begin to become yours.

PROVERBS 3:5-6 | *Trust in the LORD with all your heart; do not depend on your own understanding. Seek his will in all you do, and he will show you which path to take.*

MATTHEW 6:33 | *Seek the Kingdom of God above all else, and live righteously, and he will give you everything you need.*

MATTHEW 16:25 | *[Jesus said,] "If you try to hang on to your life, you will lose it. But if you give up your life for my sake, you will save it."*

If you make time with God your first priority of the day, you will find that he will give you perspective on your activities for the rest of the day and a greater desire to obey him as you see the rewards of obedience. Ask God to show you what is worth being concerned about, and then you won't lose your perspective.

PRAYER

. . . to submit to God as the Power who can help me, to admit to him my problem, and to thank him for continuing to love me in spite of my problem.

What is prayer?

2 CHRONICLES 7:14 | *[The Lord said,] "If my people who are called by my name will humble themselves and pray and seek my face and turn from their wicked ways, I will hear from heaven."*

PSALM 140:6 | *I said to the LORD, "You are my God!" Listen, O LORD, to my cries for mercy!*

Prayer is conversation with God. It is simply talking with God *and* listening to him, honestly telling him your thoughts and feelings, praising him, thanking him, confessing your sin, and asking for his help and advice. The essence of prayer is humbly entering the very presence of almighty God.

PSALM 38:18 | *I confess my sins; I am deeply sorry for what I have done.*

1 JOHN 1:9 | *If we confess our sins to him, he is faithful and just to forgive us our sins and to cleanse us from all wickedness.*

Prayer often begins with a confession of sin. It is through confession that you demonstrate the humility necessary for open lines of communication with the almighty, holy God.

1 SAMUEL 14:36 | *But the priest said, "Let's ask God first."*

2 SAMUEL 5:19 | *David asked the LORD, "Should I go . . . ?"*

Prayer is asking God for guidance and waiting for his direction and his leading.

MARK 1:35 | *Before daybreak the next morning, Jesus got up and went out to an isolated place to pray.*

Prayer is an expression of an intimate relationship with your heavenly Father, who makes his own love and resources available to you. Just as you enjoy being with people you love, you will enjoy spending time with God the more you get to know him and understand just how much he loves you.

1 SAMUEL 3:10 | *And the LORD came and called as before, "Samuel! Samuel!" And Samuel replied, "Speak, your servant is listening."*

Good conversation also includes listening, so make time for God to speak to you. When you listen to God, he will make his wisdom and plan known to you.

Why is prayer important?

MATTHEW 7:7-11 | *Keep on asking, and you will receive what you ask for. Keep on seeking, and you will find. Keep on knocking, and the door will be opened to you. For everyone who asks, receives. Everyone who seeks, finds. And to everyone who knocks, the door will be opened. You parents—if your children ask for a loaf of bread, do you give them a stone instead? Or if they ask for a fish, do you give them a snake? Of course not! So if you sinful people know how to give good gifts to your children, how much more will your heavenly Father give good gifts to those who ask him.*

There's more to prayer than just getting an answer to a question or a solution for a problem. God often does more in your heart through the act of prayer than he does in actually answering your prayer. As you persist in talking and listening, you often gain greater understanding of yourself, your situation, your motivation, and God's nature and direction for your life. This is the perspective you need on the journey toward recovery.

How will God respond to my prayers?

PSALM 9:12 | *[The Lord] does not ignore the cries of those who suffer.*

PSALM 55:22 | *Give your burdens to the LORD, and he will take care of you.*

1 PETER 5:7 | *Give all your worries and cares to God, for he cares about you.*

God cares for you and does not ignore a single prayer, no matter how simple it may be. When you bring your burdens to God in prayer, you will often experience real freedom from worry and anxiety in your heart and soul because you are confident he cares and is listening. The assurance of God's love and concern refreshes you and renews your hope.

PHILIPPIANS 4:6-7 | *Don't worry about anything; instead, pray about everything. Tell God what you need, and thank him for all he has done. Then you will experience God's peace, which exceeds anything we can understand. His peace will guard your hearts and minds as you live in Christ Jesus.*

There's no limit on prayer. Big requests, small requests, and all sizes in between are welcomed by God. If something is bothering you, bring it to God.

MOTIVES

. . . to really want to change now.

Why are good motives important in recovery?

1 SAMUEL 16:7 | *The LORD doesn't see things the way you see them. People judge by outward appearance, but the LORD looks at the heart.*

1 CHRONICLES 29:17 | *I know, my God, that you examine our hearts and rejoice when you find integrity there. You know I have done all this with good motives.*

PSALM 119:40 | *I long to obey your commandments! Renew my life with your goodness.*

PROVERBS 20:27 | *The LORD's light penetrates the human spirit, exposing every hidden motive.*

PHILIPPIANS 3:10 | *I want to know Christ and experience the mighty power that raised him from the dead.*

In the recovery process, you must really *want* to change. Otherwise change won't last. That's why your motives are so important to God. He is more concerned about your motives than your appearance or outward actions because your motives determine the condition of your heart, and the condition of your heart is essential to recovery. And what do you want to change into? The person God created you to be. And how do you discover that? It's a lifelong journey of walking side by side with God as you read his words to you, the Bible, and learn to hear his voice as you talk with him every day.

MATTHEW 6:1 | *Don't do your good deeds publicly, to be admired by others, for you will lose the reward from your Father in heaven.*

When you pursue life with self-serving motives, you rob yourself of the joy God gives, because joy comes from thinking of God and others first.

How can I have purer motives?

1 CORINTHIANS 4:4 | *My conscience is clear, but that doesn't prove I'm right. It is the Lord himself who will examine me and decide.*

Remember that God alone knows your heart. Ask him to reveal to you any area in which your motives are less than pure.

PSALM 19:14 | *May the words of my mouth and the meditation of my heart be pleasing to you, O LORD, my rock and my redeemer.*

Ask God to change the way you think by changing your heart.

PSALM 26:2 | *Put me on trial, LORD, and cross-examine me. Test my motives and my heart.*

PROVERBS 17:3 | *Fire tests the purity of silver and gold, but the LORD tests the heart.*

2 THESSALONIANS 1:11 | *We keep on praying for you, asking our God to enable you to live a life worthy of his call. May he give you the power to accomplish all the good things your faith prompts you to do.*

Welcome it when God tests your motives. This gives you an opportunity to grow. It is hard to resist temptation if your motives are bad, but you will find that that the more you resist something that is tempting, the better your motives become. This is because not only do you know that you should be resisting temptation, but your strengthened motives will help you actually not want to do what you once did.

CONVICTIONS

. . . to determine the way I really want to live and what I must do to achieve that.

What would my life be like without convictions?

JUDGES 21:25 | *In those days . . . the people did whatever seemed right in their own eyes.*

DANIEL 3:7 | *At the sound of the musical instruments, all the people, whatever their race or nation or language, bowed to the ground and worshiped the gold statue that King Nebuchadnezzar had set up.*

1 TIMOTHY 1:19 | *Cling to your faith in Christ, and keep your conscience clear. For some people have deliberately violated their consciences; as a result, their faith has been shipwrecked.*

TITUS 1:15 | *Everything is pure to those whose hearts are pure. But nothing is pure to those who are corrupt and unbelieving, because their minds and consciences are corrupted.*

Without godly, personal convictions, you have no guidelines for living. And with no guidelines for living, it is impossible to live for God. You will end up doing what seems right in your own eyes rather than what God wants. And that will lead to separation from him, which will keep you from experiencing eternal life with him.

How can I develop stronger convictions?

PROVERBS 2:8-9 | *[The Lord] guards the paths of the just and protects those who are faithful to him. Then you will understand what is right, just, and fair, and you will find the right way to go.*

GALATIANS 5:16-17 | *Let the Holy Spirit guide your lives. Then you won't be doing what your sinful nature craves. The sinful nature wants to do evil, which is just the opposite of what the Spirit wants. And the Spirit gives us desires that are the opposite of what the sinful nature desires.*

Every day you are faced with many opportunities to choose right from wrong, good from bad, God's way or the way of the world. Practice choosing God's way. Be tenacious about not letting Satan take over any territory in your heart. Be committed to winning even the little battles.

ISAIAH 51:7 | *Listen to me, you who know right from wrong, you who cherish my law in your hearts. Do not be afraid of people's scorn, nor fear their insults.*

Be committed to knowing God's Word, the Bible, so that you can obey it. Do not be intimidated when others make fun of you for living by the principles of the Bible, for this is the only way to live free of the things that try to control you.

PSALM 37:30 | *The godly offer good counsel; they teach right from wrong.*

Get advice from godly people who have demonstrated wisdom. They can encourage you and hold you accountable to your convictions.

SURRENDER

. . . to be completely willing to give up my own way of doing things and truly desire to follow God's way of doing things.

In the battles of life, when is it wise to surrender?

MARK 8:34 | *[Jesus] said, "If any of you wants to be my follower, you must turn from your selfish ways, take up your cross, and follow me."*

LUKE 14:33 | *You cannot become my disciple without giving up everything you own.*

ROMANS 6:4, 6, 8 | *We died and were buried with Christ by baptism. And just as Christ was raised from the dead by the glorious power of the Father, now we also may live new lives. . . . Our old sinful selves were crucified with Christ so that sin might lose its power in our lives. We are no longer slaves to sin. . . . And since we died with Christ, we know we will also live with him.*

PHILIPPIANS 3:8 | *Everything else is worthless when compared with the infinite value of knowing Christ Jesus my Lord. For his sake I have discarded everything else, counting it all as garbage, so that I could gain Christ.*

Many great battles in history concluded with surrender. One side realized they were powerless against the other, and to save themselves they admitted defeat and raised a white flag. In the spiritual realm, you fight two great battles, and surrender plays a part in both. On the one hand, you fight against sin and its control in your life. If you are not allied with God, you will surrender to sin and its deadly consequences. On the other hand, you often foolishly fight against God and his will for you because you want to have ultimate control over your life. This is a time when surrender is necessary and positive. Surrender to God comes when you at last realize you are powerless to defeat sin by yourself and you give control of your life to God. It is when you are in alliance with God that you are able to be victorious in your battle to defeat sin and gain victory over your temptations.

HOPE

. . . to really believe that I can do this, that recovery is possible, and that a new way of living for God will bring long-term joy.

How can hope for the future help me recover?

ROMANS 8:18, 21, 23-25 | *What we suffer now is nothing compared to the glory he will reveal to us later. . . . The creation looks forward to the day when it will join God's children in glorious freedom from death and decay. . . . And we believers . . . groan, even though we have the Holy Spirit within us as a foretaste of future glory, for we long for our bodies to be released from sin and suffering. We, too, wait with eager hope for the day when God will give us our full rights as his adopted children, including the new bodies he has promised us. We were given this hope when we were saved. (If we already have something, we don't need to hope for it. But if we look forward to something we don't yet have, we must wait patiently and confidently.)*

If you put your hope in God, you can put heaven and earth in perspective. On earth, you will probably live less than a hundred years. In heaven, one hundred million years is just the beginning. This eternal perspective helps you live with the right priorities, in spite of the pain and heartache that life often throws at you. Hope gives you the strength and courage to face this life because you can look beyond it to the glory that God has in store for you. So you know you can do this. Recovery is possible, and along with it a life of freedom and joy.

PHILIPPIANS 3:13 | *I focus on this one thing: Forgetting the past and looking forward to what lies ahead.*

1 PETER 5:10 | *After you have suffered a little while, he will restore, support, and strengthen you, and he will place you on a firm foundation.*

Hope is a key motivating factor to help you resist temptation so that you can recover more quickly.

How can I develop stronger hope?

EPHESIANS 3:20 | *All glory to God, who is able, through his mighty power at work within us, to accomplish infinitely more than we might ask or think.*

Most people hope too little in God and expect too little from him. If you remind yourself of the amazing things God has already done, you will know that the sovereign Lord of the universe wants to bless you more abundantly than you can imagine.

JOHN 14:1 | *[Jesus said,] "Don't let your hearts be troubled. Trust in God, and trust also in me."*

JOHN 16:33 | *[Jesus said,] "Have peace in me. Here on earth you will have many trials and sorrows. But take heart, because I have overcome the world."*

Your troubles do not surprise God and should not surprise you. Trouble is a fact of life in this broken world. Your focus should be on Jesus, who experienced the same troubles you have experienced and shows you how to have peace in spite of them.

FAITH

. . . to know that God wants to heal me and to trust that God is going to be with me every step of the way in my recovery journey.

How can I have faith that I will recover?

PSALM 119:30 | *I have chosen to be faithful; I have determined to live by your regulations.*

PSALM 119:48, 54 | *I honor and love your commands. I meditate on your decrees. . . . Your decrees have been the theme of my songs wherever I have lived.*

ROMANS 10:17 | *Faith comes from hearing, that is, hearing the Good News about Christ.*

Faith comes from reading God's Word. Your faith will grow stronger as you study the Bible, reflect on its truths, and see how obeying it changes your life.

JOHN 20:27-29 | *[Jesus] said to Thomas, "Put your finger here, and look at my hands. Put your hand into the wound in my side. Don't be faithless any longer. Believe!" "My Lord and my God!" Thomas exclaimed. Then Jesus told him, "You believe because you have seen me. Blessed are those who believe without seeing me."*

2 CORINTHIANS 3:14 | *The people's minds were hardened, and to this day whenever the old covenant is being read, the same veil covers their minds so they cannot understand the truth. And this veil can be removed only by believing in Christ.*

Faith is not based on physical senses but on spiritual conviction. Your faith will become stronger the more you ask God to strengthen it.

LUKE 5:12-13 | *"Lord," [the man] said, "if you are willing, you can heal me . . ." Jesus reached out and touched him. "I am willing," he said. "Be healed!"*

Jesus has the ability and the willingness to heal you. You are not bothering him when you pray for healing; you are expressing your faith and trust in him. For reasons known only to God, Jesus doesn't heal all your health problems or all your addictions at once, but he does perform great acts of healing in you every day—healing you from sin, grief, hopelessness, and weariness of soul.

COURAGE

. . . to get started in fighting my problem and/or addiction.

How do I find the courage to face change?

GENESIS 46:3 | *Do not be afraid to go . . .*

Change will be part of God's plan for you. What you are headed into will give you joy and satisfaction beyond your expectations. Remember, the greatest advances in life come through change. But you need courage to take the first step.

2 SAMUEL 4:1 | *When Ishbosheth, Saul's son, heard about Abner's death at Hebron, he lost all courage, and all Israel became paralyzed with fear.*

If you lean on another person for courage, you will be left with nothing when that person is gone. If you trust in God for courage, you will have the strength to go on even when circumstances collapse around you, because God is always there and never changes.

Where do I get the courage to recover?

DEUTERONOMY 20:1 | *The LORD your God . . . is with you!*

JOSHUA 1:9 | *Be strong and courageous! Do not be afraid or discouraged. For the LORD your God is with you wherever you go.*

PSALM 27:1 | *The LORD is my light and my salvation—so why should I be afraid?*

ISAIAH 41:10 | *Don't be afraid, for I am with you. Don't be discouraged, for I am your God. I will strengthen you and help you. I will hold you up with my victorious right hand.*

Fear comes from feeling alone against a threat. Courage comes from knowing God is beside you helping you fight the threat. To stay courageous, focus more on his presence and less on the problem.

JEREMIAH 23:24 | *"Can anyone hide from me in a secret place? Am I not everywhere in all the heavens and earth?" says the* LORD.

NAHUM 1:7 | *The* LORD *is good, a strong refuge when trouble comes. He is close to those who trust in him.*

Go to God honestly. Realize that he already knows what you think and what you have done, but the process of admitting these things to him is important. Courage begins when you admit that you need someone's help, and who can help you more than God? Go to him first. He may show you others who can help as well.

PSALM 19:12 | *How can I know all the sins lurking in my heart? Cleanse me from these hidden faults.*

HEBREWS 4:12 | *The word of God is alive and powerful. It is sharper than the sharpest two-edged sword, cutting between soul and spirit, between joint and marrow. It exposes our innermost thoughts and desires.*

God's Word shines a light on the sins lurking in the dark corners of your life. Only when you have the courage to stop hiding your sins can you be released from their power to control you.

VISION

. . . to make a plan to recover, imagining myself recovered down the road and beginning to see how to get there.

Why is vision an important trait for recovery?

PSALM 119:18 | *Open my eyes to see . . .*

EPHESIANS 3:20 | *All glory to God, who is able, through his mighty power at work within us, to accomplish infinitely more than we might ask or think.*

Vision is a picture of the future that gives you a passion for something right now. Lack of vision is like trying to see underwater without a mask—everything is blurry, nothing makes sense, and you feel completely lost. If you want to have purpose, if you want to clearly see your way in life, if you want to be motivated to do something that counts, you need vision—a picture of where you'd like to be at some point in the future. Spiritual vision is the picture of the future God created for you. How do you capture God's vision of where he wants you to be and what he created you to accomplish? It's only when you empty yourself of your own opinions, addictions, and desires that God can fill you up with his picture of what he wants for you. Then the recovery process becomes an exciting journey to the place God wants you to go.

ZECHARIAH 8:4-6 | *This is what the LORD of Heaven's Armies says: Once again old men and women will walk Jerusalem's streets with their canes and will sit together in the city squares. And the streets of the city will be filled with boys and girls at play. This*

is what the LORD of Heaven's Armies says: All this may seem
impossible to you now, a small remnant of God's people. But is
it impossible for me? says the LORD of Heaven's Armies.

ZECHARIAH 8:9 | *This is what the LORD of Heaven's Armies says:*
Be strong and finish the task!

Having a vision helps you get things moving and get things
done. The Temple in Jerusalem still needed to be rebuilt
after long years of exile, but the people weren't motivated
to finish it. God gave Zechariah a vision of the city of
Jerusalem once again filled with joyful people, and that
vision, in turn, motivated the people to complete their task.
Ask God to give you a vision not only for when you are fully
recovered but also of the steps you need to take to recover.
Envision goals that you can meet, and make plans for how
you will meet them.

ECCLESIASTES 1:8 | *Everything is wearisome beyond description.*
No matter how much we see, we are never satisfied. No matter
how much we hear, we are not content.

Living in a state of constant weariness can blur your vision
and your purpose. It is hard to look ahead when you feel
you can't go on. That is where God comes in. Ask him to
help you view life from his perspective. He does not resent
your asking, and in fact, he longs to grant your request.

MOTIVATION

. . . to develop specific ideas that can encourage me to keep
going in the right direction.

How can I stay motivated to keep going in the right direction?

JEREMIAH 20:9 I *If I say I'll never mention the LORD or speak in his name, his word burns in my heart like a fire. It's like a fire in my bones! I am worn out trying to hold it in! I can't do it!*

ACTS 20:24 I *My life is worth nothing to me unless I use it for finishing the work assigned me by the Lord Jesus.*

ROMANS 12:2 I *Let God transform you into a new person by changing the way you think. Then you will learn to know God's will for you, which is good and pleasing and perfect.*

2 CORINTHIANS 4:1 I *Since God in his mercy has given us this new way, we never give up.*

When you nurture your relationship with God, work, blessings, commands, and calling become like a burning passion within. Even when you try to resist them or escape, you cannot. The closer you are to God, the more he motivates you with a clear, ever-growing vision for your future and your part in his eternal plan. Often, lack of motivation comes from lack of purpose. But God's purposes infuse your life with energy and confidence as you trust in him. When you're feeling discouraged because outward circumstances threaten to crush you, let your sense of God's presence, God's call, and God's love sustain you. By focusing on these things, you secure God's purpose in your mind and heart, pushing you to fulfill all he has planned for you. It is through anticipation for your future that you are compelled to move forward today.

How do I stay motivated when I get discouraged?

MATTHEW 6:33 | *Seek the Kingdom of God above all else, and live righteously, and he will give you everything you need.*

Does God really promise to provide what you need if you live for him? Yes! What better motivation is there to recover than to know that if you make God your first priority, you will have his love and support, and you will be following his plan for your future?

2 CORINTHIANS 1:4 | *He comforts us in all our troubles so that we can comfort others. When they are troubled, we will be able to give them the same comfort God has given us.*

Motivation can also be revived by realizing that once you recover you can help others to do the same.

SELF-CONTROL

. . . to develop the discipline to keep following the plan once it goes into action and to find someone who will keep me account-able to stay on course.

How can I have the self-control needed to recover?

GALATIANS 5:24 | *Those who belong to Christ Jesus have nailed the passions and desires of their sinful nature to his cross and crucified them there.*

2 PETER 1:5-6 | *Supplement your faith with a generous provision of moral excellence, and moral excellence with knowledge, and knowledge with self-control, and self-control with patient endurance, and patient endurance with godliness.*

According to the Bible, sin will control your life until you let Jesus Christ break its power. Only then can you live the way God intended. When you have put your faith in Jesus Christ, you can tap into a whole new power source that will help you control unhealthy desires and live in a way that brings real joy and freedom.

1 CORINTHIANS 9:25 | *All athletes are disciplined in their training. They do it to win a prize that will fade away, but we do it for an eternal prize.*

1 TIMOTHY 4:7-10 | *Train yourself to be godly. Physical training is good, but training for godliness is much better, promising benefits in this life and in the life to come. This is a trustworthy saying, and everyone should accept it. This is why we work hard and continue to struggle, for our hope is in the living God, who is the Savior of all people and particularly of all believers.*

Self-control begins with God's work in you, but it requires your effort as well. Just as musicians and athletes must develop their talent, strength, and coordination through intentional effort, spiritual fitness must be intentional as well. You can do this by (1) honestly assessing your weaknesses, (2) determining that they will no longer rule you, (3) appealing to the Holy Spirit to help you stand strong against temptation, (4) humbly confessing to God when you make a mistake, and (5) thanking God every time he helps you resist temptation.

1 CORINTHIANS 10:13 | *God is faithful. He will not allow the temptation to be more than you can stand. When you are tempted, he will show you a way out so that you can endure.*

The Bible makes it clear that temptation can always be resisted. It might be hard, but temptation will never be more than you can handle. This is because God will help you see the way out of it if you ask. Many times you knew you should resist but you still didn't. Have you ever wondered, *after* you fell into temptation, why you hadn't looked for the way out? Try taking the high road next time. It will surprise you how much power you have over temptation, and it will encourage you to know you can resist next time.

How can I cultivate discipline?

DEUTERONOMY 11:18-19, 22 | *Commit yourselves wholeheartedly to these words. . . . Tie them to your hands and wear them on your forehead as reminders. Teach them to your children. Talk about them when you are at home and when you are on the road, when you are going to bed and when you are getting up. . . . Be careful to obey all these commands. . . . Show love to the LORD your God by walking in his ways and holding tightly to him.*

1 PETER 4:7 | *Be earnest and disciplined in your prayers.*

It is difficult for most of us to make obedience a habit because we are often tempted to give in to those sins that we enjoy the most and because we, by nature, want our own way. Here are three principles in the discipline of obedience: (1) Pray, read the Bible, and meditate on it daily; (2) keep a spiritual diary or journal, writing down commands that God wants you to obey; and (3) each day, find an opportunity to practice doing one thing out of obedience to God. If you follow these principles every day, you will come to love obeying God, and it will be a lot easier to recover.

CONFIDENCE

. . . to trust that the plan will work.

How can I have confidence that I will recover?

1 PETER 5:7 | *Give all your worries and cares to God, for he cares about you.*

The God who created the universe created you and truly cares about you. Because he cares so deeply about you, he is working right now to help you.

ROMANS 8:38-39 | *Nothing can ever separate us from God's love. Neither death nor life, neither angels nor demons, neither our fears for today nor our worries about tomorrow —not even the powers of hell can separate us from God's love. No power in the sky above or in the earth below— indeed, nothing in all creation will ever be able to separate us from the love of God that is revealed in Christ Jesus our Lord.*

God assures you in his Word that even the powers of hell cannot keep you from experiencing the benefits of his love.

PSALM 112:6-8 | *Those who are righteous will be long remembered. They do not fear bad news; they confidently trust the LORD to care for them. They are confident and fearless and can face their foes triumphantly.*

There is something about having a clear conscience that gives one confidence. Have you ever resisted doing something you knew was wrong and then experienced joy in your victory? This gives you even more confidence the next time that temptation comes around that you can overcome it.

PHILIPPIANS 4:13 | *I can do everything through Christ, who gives me strength.*

No matter what situation you find yourself in, God promises to give you the help and strength you need. Have confidence that your plan to recover will work, because God is going to help you through it.

TRUST

. . . to believe that God will help the plan work.

Why should I trust God that I will recover?

JEREMIAH 29:11 | *"I know the plans I have for you," says the LORD. "They are plans for good and not for disaster, to give you a future and a hope."*

God's plans are always for your good, so you can trust that he wants you to fully recover. His desires for you will fulfill and satisfy you. If your mind and heart are truly in tune with his will, you won't be going where you don't want to go—he changes your heart so you will want what he has planned for you. But you must let him change your heart.

PSALM 62:8 | *O my people, trust in him at all times. Pour out your heart to him, for God is our refuge.*

PSALM 143:8 | *Let me hear of your unfailing love each morning, for I am trusting you. Show me where to walk, for I give myself to you.*

Trust that God has everything under control. He will not let you fail in life if you accept his plans to help you.

EPHESIANS 2:10 | *We are God's masterpiece. He has created us anew in Christ Jesus, so we can do the good things he planned for us long ago.*

PHILIPPIANS 1:6 | *God, who began the good work within you, will continue his work until it is finally finished.*

We can trust that the God who made us wants us to recover and become the persons he created us to be. When we trust in our own strength, we may slip and fall. But God cannot fail—and he has promised to keep working in us until we are complete. We are his masterpieces, not rejects and failures.

PATIENCE

. . . to accept that it will take time for full recovery to happen.

How can I be patient when my recovery isn't going as quickly as I'd like?

HEBREWS 10:36 | *Patient endurance is what you need now, so that you will continue to do God's will. Then you will receive all that he has promised.*

Knowing the purposes for your recovery is the key to patience. Once you have fully recovered, you can tell others your story to help them recover as well. An important reason to recover is to have a goal for your own life. And by knowing that your long-range future is totally secure, you can be more patient with today's frustrations.

PSALM 37:34 | *Put your hope in the LORD. Travel steadily along his path.*

ROMANS 8:25 | *If we look forward to something we don't yet have, we must wait patiently and confidently.*

JAMES 5:7-8 | *Consider the farmers who patiently wait for the rains in the fall and in the spring. They eagerly look for the valuable harvest to ripen. You, too, must be patient.*

Goals are rarely achieved by quantum leaps, but rather in small increments. Patience comes from taking small, faithful steps toward your goals and holding on to hope when circumstances seem to block your way. Whether you're waiting for crops to ripen, a child to mature, God to perfect you, or a traffic jam to unsnarl, you can grow in patience by recognizing that learning patience takes time and there is only so much you can do to help it along. In fact, it is only through persevering and enduring frustrating circumstances that you will develop patience. When you're going through hard times, the hope you have in God's plans for your life, especially his eternal plans, can help you take faithful steps to bring you to the other side. When you know that your eternal future is secure, you can grow in patience through today's frustrations.

ROMANS 5:3-5 | *We can rejoice, too, when we run into problems and trials, for we know that they help us develop endurance. And endurance develops strength of character, and character strengthens our confident hope of salvation. And this hope will not lead to disappointment. For we know how dearly God loves us, because he has given us the Holy Spirit to fill our hearts with his love.*

This world is God's waiting room. While you wait, you learn better how to trust. You gain endurance, strength, humility, and a deepening appreciation for God's care in your life by being patient while waiting for full recovery.

ENDURANCE

. . . to keep at it and never give up so that the goal will be reached.

How do I keep going when the urge to give up is so strong?

2 CORINTHIANS 1:8-9 | *We were crushed and overwhelmed beyond our ability to endure, and we thought we would never live through it. In fact, we expected to die. But as a result, we stopped relying on ourselves and learned to rely only on God, who raises the dead.*

COLOSSIANS 1:10-11 | *You will grow as you learn to know God better and better. We . . . pray that you will be strengthened with all his glorious power so you will have all the endurance and patience you need. May you be filled with joy.*

2 THESSALONIANS 3:5 | *May the Lord lead your hearts into a full understanding and expression of the love of God and the patient endurance that comes from Christ.*

The fuel of endurance for life is the power of God working through you. Not only do you simply have to ask for endurance, but the more obedient and in tune you are with God, the more his power will strengthen your ability to endure.

JOHN 14:2 I *[Jesus said,] "There is more than enough room in my Father's home. If this were not so, would I have told you that I am going to prepare a place for you?"*

GALATIANS 6:9 I *Let's not get tired of doing what is good. At just the right time we will reap a harvest of blessing if we don't give up.*

1 THESSALONIANS 1:3 I *As we pray to our God and Father about you, we think of your faithful work, your loving deeds, and the enduring hope you have because of our Lord Jesus Christ.*

You can avoid discouragement and the desire to quit by thinking about heaven. Remember that in this life you will face many problems, but in the life to come they will all be gone forever (see John 16:33; Revelation 21:4). This hope gives you endurance to go on.

2 CORINTHIANS 8:10-11 I *It would be good for you to finish what you started a year ago. Last year you were the first who wanted to give, and you were the first to begin doing it. Now you should finish what you started. Let the eagerness you showed in the beginning be matched now.*

Perseverance involves setting manageable goals that keep you on track to finish what you started. You can resist quitting when you keep yourself focused on accomplishing your goals one step at a time.

ROMANS 5:3 I *We can rejoice, too, when we run into problems and trials, for we know that they help us develop endurance.*

JAMES 1:2-4 I *When troubles come your way, consider it an opportunity for great joy. For you know that when your faith is tested, your endurance has a chance to grow. So let it grow, for when your endurance is fully developed, you will be perfect and complete, needing nothing.*

Problems, trials, troubles, and the testing of your faith can help you become either weaker or stronger. If you see your problems as giant barriers, you will get discouraged and turn back, never allowing yourself to become more than you are now. But if you see defeating your problems as a way to become stronger, you can move ahead with anticipation for what you will become—a person who can resist every obstacle that comes around with more ease than the previous one. This is a key realization for recovery.

JOHN 15:5 | *Those who remain in me, and I in them, will produce much fruit.*

GALATIANS 6:9 | *Let's not get tired of doing what is good. At just the right time we will reap a harvest of blessing if we don't give up.*

EPHESIANS 3:20 | *All glory to God, who is able, through his mighty power at work within us, to accomplish infinitely more than we might ask or think.*

The 12-step recovery program gives you an advantage over most people. Learning to endure through a program like this is not how most people learn the art of perseverance. Once you have recovered, your strong-built endurance will help you conquer whatever else life throws at you. Think of how productive your life will be once you are recovered!

PROVERBS 4:27 | *Don't get sidetracked; keep your feet from following evil.*

To endure, avoid distractions. Distractions lead you away from the goals you have set. The easiest way to avoid distractions is to walk away from them the moment you recognize the temptation. The longer you think about a distraction, the more likely it is you will succumb to it.

THANKFULNESS

. . . to God and others for a new lease on life and the victories along the way.

How can I thank God when life is difficult?

GENESIS 50:19-20 | *Joseph [said], "Don't be afraid of me. Am I God, that I can punish you? You intended to harm me, but God intended it all for good."*

1 THESSALONIANS 5:18 | *Be thankful in all circumstances, for this is God's will for you who belong to Christ Jesus.*

REVELATION 21:4 | *[God] will wipe every tear from their eyes, and there will be no more death or sorrow or crying or pain. All these things are gone forever.*

Life can be difficult for many reasons. You may experience the consequences of your own mistakes, you may struggle on your road to recovery, you may be caught in circumstances that are no one's fault but are nonetheless unfortunate. God may be testing your faith or you may be a target of Satan, who wants to disrupt your godly influence and discourage you. In any of these tough circumstances, there is a reason to thank God. He redeems your mistakes, teaches you wisdom through adversity, promises to help you through tough times, and guarantees eternal life free from suffering for all his followers. A God who redeems all trouble is a God worthy of praise and thanksgiving.

What happens when I have an attitude of thankfulness?

HABAKKUK 3:17-19 | *Even though the fig trees have no blossoms, and there are no grapes on the vines; even though the olive crop fails, and the fields lie empty and barren; even though the flocks die in the fields, and the cattle barns are empty, yet I will rejoice in the LORD! I will be joyful in the God of my salvation! The Sovereign LORD is my strength!*

COLOSSIANS 2:7 | *Let your roots grow down into [Christ Jesus], and let your lives be built on him. Then your faith will grow strong in the truth you were taught, and you will overflow with thankfulness.*

A spirit of gratitude and praise changes the way you look at life. Complaining connects you to your unhappiness— gratitude and praise connect you to the source of real joy.

PSALM 50:23 | *Giving thanks is a sacrifice that truly honors me. If you keep to my path, I will reveal to you the salvation of God.*

A thankful heart gives you a positive attitude because it keeps you focused on all God is doing for you, not on what you think you lack. Make giving thanks a part of your prayer time, and thank God for something every day. That is a sacrifice of love that honors God and brings his blessing.

STABILITY

. . . to not give in to impulsive urges and to keep moving forward one step at a time.

What are the keys to finding and maintaining stability in life?

MATTHEW 7:24-27 | *[Jesus said,] "Anyone who listens to my teaching and follows it is wise, like a person who builds a house on solid rock. Though the rain comes in torrents and the floodwaters rise and the winds beat against that house, it won't collapse because it is built on bedrock. But anyone who hears my teaching and doesn't obey it is foolish, like a person who builds a house on sand. When the rains and floods come and the winds beat against that house, it will collapse with a mighty crash."*

COLOSSIANS 2:6-7 | *Just as you accepted Christ Jesus as your Lord, you must continue to follow him. Let your roots grow down into him, and let your lives be built on him. Then your faith will grow strong in the truth you were taught, and you will overflow with thankfulness.*

Stability is a condition more of the heart and mind and less of a lifestyle, which can be conditional on so many tentative factors. Stability comes from a consistently growing relationship with God, in which you base your character on what his is like.

PROVERBS 4:26 | *Mark out a straight path for your feet; stay on the safe path.*

When you are just redeveloping the stability you have lost, it may be necessary to plan out or schedule certain tasks. Perhaps purchasing a calendar can help you remember to do what you know you must, such as reading the Bible, finding a consistent time to pray, and setting goals that focus on recovery rather than on distractions. Once these things are written on your calendar, do them.

MICAH 6:8 | *The LORD has told you what is good, and this is what he requires of you: to do what is right, to love mercy, and to walk humbly with your God.*

JAMES 3:13 | *If you are wise and understand God's ways, prove it by living an honorable life, doing good works with the humility that comes from wisdom.*

1 PETER 4:19 | *Keep on doing what is right, and trust your lives to the God who created you, for he will never fail you.*

Stability means to be faithful in your habits, to regularly behave in ways that are pleasing to God and helpful to others. The Bible calls you to be consistent in your obedience to God, your faithfulness and love toward others, and your discipline of maturing in the faith. If you do these things, you will give in to impulsive urges less frequently and you will move steadily forward with your recovery, one step at a time.

RESPONSIBILITY

. . . to follow my plan and to make decisions (after getting input from others) that show I am serious about my recovery.

Am I really responsible for my actions? I can't help it when I do certain things.

ROMANS 6:12-14 | *Do not let sin control the way you live; do not give in to sinful desires. Do not let any part of your body become an instrument of evil to serve sin. Instead, give your- selves completely to God, for you were dead, but now you have new life. So use your whole body as an instrument to do what is right for the glory of God. Sin is no longer your master, for you no longer live under the requirements of the law. Instead, you live under the freedom of God's grace.*

ROMANS 6:16 | *Don't you realize that you become the slave of whatever you choose to obey? You can be a slave to sin, which leads to death, or you can choose to obey God, which leads to righteous living.*

The term *bad habit* perhaps brings to mind such things as smoking, drinking too much alcohol, and taking drugs. But spreading gossip, complaining, and backbiting are bad habits too. Worrying is another bad habit that hurts you physically and spiritually. One of Satan's great lies is that you are a victim who has no power to resist your impulses. The world teaches that heredity, environment, and circum- stances excuse you from responsibility. In reality, everything you do is the result of a choice you make, and you are responsible for every choice you make. Yes, it's hard to resist certain temptations and to always make good choices. But you have no one to blame for bad choices but yourself. The good news is that God is more powerful than anything that seeks to control you. When you tap into his power through prayer and use the support of fellow believers, God breaks the chains that hold you and you develop the discipline to say no. This shows that you are serious about your recovery.

What is the benefit of responsibility?

GENESIS 41:1, 14, 39-40 | *Later . . . Pharaoh sent for Joseph . . . and he was quickly brought from the prison. . . . Then Pharaoh said to Joseph, "Since God has revealed the meaning of the dreams to you, clearly no one else is as intelligent or wise as you are. You will be in charge of my court, and all my people will take orders from you. Only I, sitting on my throne, will have a rank higher than yours."*

EPHESIANS 5:16 | *Make the most of every opportunity in these evil days.*

Taking responsibility opens the door to better opportunities. Joseph was unjustly thrown into prison (see Genesis 39:6-20). He could have whined and complained, become bitter, or just given up. Instead, he did the right thing even in an unfair situation, and he became trusted for his responsibility, eventually rising to great prominence in Egypt. If life seems to have dealt with you unfairly, continue to do what you know is right and to do whatever you can to help others. Your good and helpful deeds should be a natural reflex of obedient faith in God. In time, your circumstances will change for the better.

POTENTIAL

. . . to have faith that I can become all God created me to be.

How can I achieve my God-given potential?

EPHESIANS 2:10 | *We are God's masterpiece. He has created us anew in Christ Jesus, so we can do the good things he planned for us long ago.*

PHILIPPIANS 1:6 | *God, who began the good work within you, will continue his work until it is finally finished on the day when Christ Jesus returns.*

Wasted potential is tragic. You were created in the image of a loving and holy God, which means you have the potential to reflect all his marvelous characteristics. You begin to develop your spiritual potential when you give God control of your life. The Holy Spirit then comes to live in your heart and begins the work of helping you reach the spiritual potential for which you were created—to reflect God's holiness and to use your spiritual gifts in helping others. Your potential is actually what God can do through you, not what you could do by yourself. Deciding not to follow God to complete recovery is deciding not to live to the potential for which you were created.

PHILIPPIANS 3:12-14 | *I don't mean to say that I have already . . . reached perfection. . . . No, dear brothers and sisters, I have not achieved it, but I focus on this one thing: Forgetting the past and looking forward to what lies ahead, I press on to reach the end of the race and receive the heavenly prize for which God, through Christ Jesus, is calling us.*

The bad news is that you will never realize your full potential on this earth because your human nature is sinful and therefore you can't be perfect. But God promises that you have far more potential than you think and that you can achieve much more than you think you can if you let him work through you. Reaching your God-given potential will not happen overnight, but it can happen with small, steady steps every day in the right direction.

1 PETER 2:9 I *You are . . . chosen . . . God's very own possession. As a result, you can show others the goodness of God, for he called you out of the darkness into his wonderful light.*

God calls out the best in you, and he sees more in you than you see in yourself. You look at your weaknesses and limitations, but God looks at your potential. If you want to change your perspective, learn to see life from God's eyes. He doesn't put nearly as many limitations on you as you do. He sees you for what he intended you to be as well as for what you are. So have faith that you can be all God created you to be, and then you can look forward to full recovery with great anticipation.

Find Healing in God's Word Every Day.

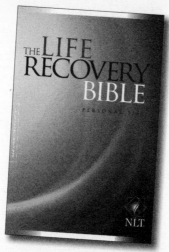

The Life Recovery Bible is today's best-selling Bible for people in recovery. In the accurate and easy-to-understand New Living Translation, *The Life Recovery Bible* leads people to the true source of healing—God himself. Special features created by two of today's leading recovery experts—David Stoop, Ph.D., and Stephen Arterburn, M.Ed.—include the following:

Twelve Step Devotionals: A reading chain of Bible-based devotionals tied to the Twelve Steps of recovery.

Serenity Prayer Devotionals: Based on the Serenity Prayer, these devotionals are placed next to the verses from which they are drawn.

Recovery Principle Devotionals: Bible-based devotionals, arranged topically, are a guide to key recovery principles.

Find *The Life Recovery Bible* at your local Christian bookstore or wherever books are sold. Learn more at www.NewLivingTranslation.com.

Available editions:
Hardcover 978-1-4143-0962-0
Softcover 978-1-4143-0961-3
Bonded Burgundy 978-1-4143-0963-7
Personal Size Softcover 978-1-4143-1626-0

CP0107